SEASONS

of

PARENTING

Unlock the Peace
and Power of Timing

Rick & Deb Fiechter

ISBN: 979-8-37365638-2 (Paperback)
ISBN: 979-8-39009389-4 (Hardback)

Cover design by Ruben Santa-Cruz
Book formatting by Emily Santa-Cruz
Editing by Jake & Jearene Webb

Printed in the United States of America
Rick and Deb Fiechter
Saint Cloud FL 34769
rick@connectionchurch.net

—

To our

five children and spouses

and their nine children

and their children's children . . .

CONTENTS

FOREWORD

As a direct result of the parenting strategies outlined in this book, I can't think of anyone better to write this foreword than one of the real-life products of the *Seasons of Parenting* principles. My name is Justin Fiechter, one of Rick and Deb's five children. Not only did my parents utilize this parenting method on me, but now my wife Shelby and I have the honor of being able to implement these parenting methods with my three children: Tessa (6), Emmie (5), and Myles (2).

The powerful truths you'll discover in the following pages of this book will be crucial to your children's development, your personal relationship with them, and your desire to see them follow and live for the Lord. You will find deeper understanding, practical application, and tangible steps outlined as you embark on the *Seasons of Parenting*.

I pray you find the success and encouragement you are seeking in the chapters to come.

—Justin Fiechter

INTRODUCTION

If you are reading this book, I'm guessing you have children and you are striving to be the best parent you can to raise godly, successful kids! We all know this can be challenging and sometimes confusing. In *Seasons of Parenting*, we are going to share with you a simple concept that when you understand and apply it to your family, will bring you the peace and confidence you are searching for in your parenting journey.

It's actually a concept that I (Rick) learned when I used to be a farmer. I grew up through a long line of farmers; my dad farmed, and so did his dad and his dad! There is a law of farming that never bends. You cannot change it and you cannot break it . . . that is, if you wish to continue farming in any successful way. It goes like this:

The right thing at the wrong time is the wrong thing.

Something right like planting seed corn in farming or gardening isn't right if it's done in the fall rather than the spring; or it would be silly to try to harvest that crop in the spring when you need to be planting—all good things, but the variable is *when* they are done. It's *the law of seasons*. Ecclesiastes 3:1 says, "For everything there is a season" and that is true for parenting as well. Without recognizing this, parents can be more frustrated, overwhelmed, conflicted, and realizing consequences that could be avoided by applying these seasonal principles.

Once you understand the seasons of parenting and the corresponding focuses, it brings clarity and assurance. So often we feel pressured or guilty for not doing everything. Or we can simply be confused because of all the information piled on us. Hopefully, once you see the overall picture then you can relax with increased insight and understanding. When you realize, "Oh, friendship comes here, discipline comes here, choices are here!" That gives you confidence. But when you try to do these "right" things at the wrong time, it gets chaotic.

Deb and I have intentionally waited until all five of our children were grown and through all of these seasons to write this book. We have gained a lot of perspective looking back on various seasons, realizing what we've done right, what we've done wrong and what we would change; it's that 20/20 hindsight thing! In some cases, our adult kids have helped us see that. We've definitely had plenty of challenges and done plenty of things wrong—we've sinned and messed up and so have our kids. Thankfully, through it all, today all five of our kids love the Lord, they love the church, and we actually enjoy hanging out together, most of the time! By God's grace, it seems to be working out.

Now that our youngest is 25, and all five of them gave us their blessing and support to write this book, we decided to give it our best shot to capture these principles that will hopefully help younger parents along the way. Deb and I are both writing this together; much of it will be me (Rick) writing but there are sections she will write. Sometimes we will clarify, but you can always know it's a joint effort together, just like parenting!

FOUR SEASONS

Much like the seasons of the year, we have broken up parenting into four seasons:

Spring (0-6)
Summer (7-12)
Fall (13-17)
Winter (18+)

The age ranges are approximations rather than technically exact times, but interestingly, these timeframes are already naturally broken down in our culture. Our children begin schooling around 5-6 years old as spring transitions to summer with its teaching focus. The teenage years, which parallel the fall harvest season, are when the child transitions into an adult and puberty happens much as the fruit and seed is harvested and ready to reproduce in farming. 18 is the age when a child is legally an adult—however much we don't want to believe it—and we as parents enter into the winter season of parenting.

All of these seasons happen in all of our children's lives no matter what we do. If we understand them and embrace them in the best way possible, doing the right thing in the right season, it can make a tremendous difference in our children's lives, and our lives as parents too—*you can experience peace in parenting!*

When I used to farm, it was easy to think about the seasons because they came every three months—cycling every year. But in parenting, each season comes only once and doesn't last three months, but six years! Because of that, each one is very important because once they pass, they are past, at least for that particular child. Trying to go backwards only confuses and confounds the challenges. Once you realize which areas to focus on and at what time, you will find clarity and freedom. Getting this understanding and embracing this concept can actually be life changing! We have seen this over and over with parents when they begin to focus on the particular season their child or children are in.

Deb and I have experienced this in so many ways throughout the years ourselves. We have seen the wonderful results of doing the right thing at the right time, and we have also seen the challenges with parenting when we and other parents did not understand these principles and tried to do the spring planting season activities during the fall season or vice-versa. Also, and almost miraculously, we have seen things change quickly and dramatically in parents and children's lives when parents stop doing the right thing at the wrong time and start doing the right thing at the right time! It is our hope and prayer that this book will give some new ideas and inspire you as you walk through the seasons of parenting with your own children.

OUTLINE OF THE BOOK

As just described with parenting, this book is also broken into four large sections, or seasons. Utilizing the metaphor of farming, each section will deal with one of the seasons of parenting:

Season I: Spring Planting—Heart & Obedience. (0-6)
Season 2: Summer Cultivating—Teaching & Vision. (7-12)
Season 3: Fall Harvest—Encouragement & Releasing. (13-17)
Season 4: Winter Reward—Rest and Friendship. (18+)

Within these sections will be chapters dealing with key emphases and activities that are best carried out during that specific season. Wherever you are at in parenting, this will be helpful—for one, you cannot go back in seasons, and in fact, trying to do so can create more challenges than good. It will be helpful for you to realize that like trying to plant the seed corn in the fall—in some cases, it is better to do nothing than to do the "right thing at the wrong time."

As you read this, you may be tempted to look backwards and overanalyze if you did or didn't do something right. We all do that, looking back and wishing we'd have learned something sooner. The best thing to always do is *jump right into the season you are in.* I love what Paul said, "One thing I do, forgetting the past and straining toward the future, I press on . . ." (Philippians 3:13).

HOW TO APPROACH THIS BOOK

Certainly, reading a book from the front all the way through is the normal approach, however depending on where you are personally, you may find it helpful to simply go straight to the season in the book that you are living through right now with your children, particularly if you are in a difficult time in parenting.

If you find this book and you have teenagers that you are frustrated with, it may be helpful to jump right into "Season 3: Fall Harvest" which are the teenage years of parenting. That is where you are living right now and may provide some practical tips or insights that may encourage you. That recently happened with a couple whose teenage son was ready to start dating and Dad and Mom were struggling with letting go and all the emotions around that; they have been soaking in that section and told us the other night that it has made a huge difference. In most of the seasons, references are made to prior focuses so then it may be helpful to go back to the beginning to get the big picture.

Or maybe you are like the dad I talked with yesterday; he and his wife just had their first little baby a month ago. I showed him this book and told him, "You are in a great place to read this from the top and gain the whole perspective!" They are just starting out.

Perhaps your kids are grown, and you are now navigating that unknown terrain of being parents of adult children. Jumping to the back "Season 4: Winter Reward" may help you right where you are. We contemplated actually breaking this up into a set of four small booklets. On one hand that may have been more directly applicable to help parents deal with their current questions or challenges, but on the other hand it is helpful to be able to see the big picture as well.

After you have gotten some practical tools to help you where you are, it is wise to go back and read the entire book to get the overall perspective. You may read in the Spring Season for young children that limiting choices is good. This could feel narrow in a culture that encourages "expression" in everything, so it will definitely give you perspective to read all the way through to understand that you should be intentionally *giving your teens* many choices, encouraging expression even though that is a time you likely don't *feel like* doing that. Often culture or our own feelings encourage us to do the opposite thing than what is helpful in a certain season. To see the flip side in an earlier or later season gives you a better understanding because seeing the big picture always helps make sense of the individual puzzle pieces.

STUDY GUIDE

We have incorporated a *Questions for Discussion* page after each of the chapters to make this a more complete resource for you. An individual can stop and ponder these questions as you are reading through the book to better process and think through the information.

Also, the *Questions for Discussion* allows this book to be used for group studies as well. Mom's groups or small groups of parents can use this to work through together as a group study guide. If the parents all have children in a similar season, it may be a short study just covering that season or an over-all perspective covering the entire book.

By reading the chapters individually during the week, you can come back together and answer the discussion questions as a group to help facilitate and process the information, gaining perspective and insight from one another. Each chapter has approximately five to seven questions at the end. A facilitator could determine ahead of time which questions they want to ask for discussion or have individuals answer the questions that seem to impact them.

With 20 chapters, this could be approximately a 6-month study covering a chapter per week, or by covering two to three chapters per week, this could be done over a seven-to-ten-week study period. Our hope was to make this as versatile and valuable of a resource as possible without the need to purchase an additional study guide.

BE ENCOURAGED

Parenting is this challenging journey of learning! It's interesting, we can't get a driver's license or a job at McDonald's without going through interviews, training, and taking some tests—but raising little humans? Well, I think a lot of us find ourselves in that role without too much prep, and then we start trying to figure it out.

Be encouraged! It is by God's grace alone that our kids grow up following Him. There is so much grace and resilience in this process and frankly, we've probably all known kids from all types of situations who end up doing really well. As you read this, you may find things you don't agree with. That's OK. Think about it, pray about it, and at least you will have another perspective to process. There is certainly no magic formula; if anything, hopefully there are some wisdom nuggets to gain in cooperating with God's rhythms and design as kids grow up.

I want to encourage you again with this: as you read, there will be things you look back on and recognize, "Oh, I didn't do that," or "I should have done this." We've done the same thing as we've learned along the way—it's normal and everyone looks back and sees things they wish they could redo. The very best thing to do is focus on where you are—what season you are in with your children and pick it up there.

I think of the cliché, "There's more than one way to skin a cat," which now that I *do* think about it—that's a pretty rough one, and I can't even think when I've skinned the last cat? But in parenting and farming, there are a lot of approaches that work out. I remember when I used to farm, I think every farmer nearly always got some good crop at harvest time. But I did observe something; the farmers that diligently learned and applied *which activities to do on time and in the right season enjoyed a better crop.*

It's not as though the farmer creates the seed, makes the soil, controls the sunshine . . . God does all that and brings the growth. That is true in parenting and even spiritually. The apostle Paul recognized that when he said, "I planted the seed, Apollos watered it, but *God has been making it grow.*" 1 Cor. 3:6. All the farmer can do is learn to best cooperate with the built-in rhythms and seasons that God has designed. The ones that gain the wisdom and discipline to make the most of each season, typically have better results as God brings the growth. We have found that to be true in parenting as well!

That is our desire for you with this book. By gaining key insights into the right focus and timing, hopefully you will enjoy greater peace and joy throughout the journey of parenting. Most importantly, your children will have the best opportunity to thrive and excel in life and develop their own relationship with the Lord, which is what we all desire.

We hope you will use this as a "field guide" that you can return to time and again throughout the years. We have also provided key books and resources for each season that will also help you to stay focused and concentrated on doing the right thing at the right time during that often long six-year period of each season. They are introduced throughout the book, and all listed together in Appendix A at the end of the book.

Let's get farming!

SEASON I

SPRING PLANTING
(0-6 years old)

OBEDIENCE & HEART

Spring is when the farmer takes the little seed and plants it in the ground. The first order of business for any farmer is that they have to prepare the soil and take the seed and submit it to the ground, where the seed has to die. Even Jesus referred to that principle when he said, "Very truly I tell you, unless a kernel of wheat falls to the ground and dies, it remains only a single seed. But if it dies, it produces many seeds" (Jn. 12:24). The Spring Planting Season of parenting is the critical time in the child's life when they have to recognize that they are *not the authority*, but rather they are under authority, and you as parents are that authority. When that little "seed" dies to his own will, and learns that he is under authority, then the absolute best possible opportunity is given to grow and flourish!

Right beside *Obedience* is your child's *Heart* focus. As parents, you are not just looking for outward obedience, but you are paying particular attention to their heart during this young Spring Season. If you get your little guy to obey outwardly, but inwardly, his heart isn't trained to obey happily, then while you may get outward conformity, their heart isn't attended to which is critically important. It takes special attention to notice the attitudes and work with their inward person. You may tell your child, "Sit down" and he does. But one honest child said, "I may be sitting on the outside, but I'm standing on the inside!"

This is a constant challenge and during this Spring Planting Season, we focus on both sides of this coin: *Heart* and *Obedience*. When these two qualities are carefully trained between the ages of 1-6, you are well on your way to enter the Summer Cultivation Season with the healthiest little plant possible, ready to grow like crazy through summer and on to a super fall harvest.

Oh, but this runs opposite of our current permissive culture! You will feel pressure from others that this is the time for them to learn independence and self-expression. That is important—but the *wrong season*. It's coming. That's the late summer and fall. Or you will feel like your child isn't keeping up because others are competing in the cultural race to brag how their child knows trigonometry at three or physics at four! Don't sweat it—there is plenty of time for all of that. Or you may feel pressure that your child has to learn to make decisions and have choices. You are right—but *not in this season*. Everything in its right time will bring the best harvest.

Now is the time to establish *Heart* and *Obedience*, which will best prepare them to soar in the Summer Cultivation and Fall Harvest

Season! "Soar" and "Sour" look pretty similar, and the main difference is "u." You can make the difference! Spring is the time to let the child be a child—play, have fun, while living under consistent loving authority through obedience with the right heart. That is enough. If that is accomplished, they will be happy and secure, ready to grow and mature faster than ever in the other seasons with all of those positive results. No rush. Relax and stay focused on just a couple main things in each season.

SEASONS OF PARENTING

CHAPTER 1

OBEDIENCE

With so many conflicting views as well as the constant day-to-day challenge, parents can lose hope that obedience is even possible or for that matter, important. It is not only possible, but very doable! When God created the human race, everything was in perfect harmony. God created Adam and Eve and told them to rule over all creation. They had only one command to obey: stay away from that tree! Then, ugly old Serpy came slithering up challenging God's Word, "Has God really said?" "You will not surely die; you will be like God!" That sounded appealing and you know the rest of the story—Adam and Eve disobeyed and the whole world came under a curse!

Enter your little junior. Ever since that time, all cute little chubby babies come into this world with an authority problem. They all want to be in control! It's called the sinful nature—passed down from our first parents, Adam and Eve. Now, it may not become apparent right away. For the first year or so, it's primarily sleeping, eating, excreting, repeating. And that in itself can be enough to make many parents wonder what has happened to their lives?! It can be exhausting! Cute and fun for sure . . . but exhausting as well.

But then, it starts to emerge. They automatically want to be in charge. That same serpent slithers up to them and says, "Has Mom said?" Somehow, that self-will begins to emerge around that 1-year-old mark. They start learning a couple words—maybe Dada or Mama. But, for every kid, right up there in the first 10 words learned are "NO" and "MINE." Isn't it interesting—it's not "yes" and "yours." It's *your primary responsibility* to train for obedience during the Spring Season and it just happens one day at a time.

BIBLICAL BACKING

It's probably obvious but might be worth stating. Our greatest desire personally was to follow the Lord and was to raise our children to believe the Word of God and learn to trust the God of the Word. So, our constant quest is to seek to properly understand and apply what the Bible has to say. The Bible is very clear on the importance of this focus of obedience for children when it says:

> Children, obey your parents in everything, for this pleases the Lord. Colossians 3:20

When the Bible gives this command, who is actually expected to make sure this is done? Can you imagine that God intended that a little 3-year-old, or five or even 7-year-old should read this, take it upon herself and desire to do this? Of course not. It is important for them to be taught about God's Word and explain what the Bible says for parents and children—but *it's up to us as parents to take responsibility* to ensure that it happens.

Also, notice how complete God intends for this to be. It doesn't say, "Children, obey your parents randomly" Or "occasionally" or even "usually." It says, "In everything." That means it is possible to train your children to obey you in everything. Now, before you give up already, realize that this is the target, and you are always working towards that. The beauty of these seasons is that they last around six years! So, it's not all accomplished in a day.

Now, let's look at the other very familiar New Testament command regarding the importance of obedience for children:

Children, obey your parents in the Lord, for this is right. "Honor your father and mother"—which is the first commandment with a promise— "so that it may go well with you and that you may enjoy long life on the earth." Fathers, do not exasperate your children; instead, bring them up in the training and instruction of the Lord.
Ephesians 6:1-4

In this section, Paul ties obedience back to the 5th Commandment. This is the first—and only, I might add—of the 10 Commandments that had a promise attached with it. If the children learned this obedience—and later honor—then it would go well with them. Wow! Think about that for a moment. That is a beautiful incentive and recognition of just how big of a deal God sees this "kids obeying parents" to be!

Then, he points out the other side of this equation, "Fathers, do not exasperate your children." Other translations say, "Don't provoke" or "Don't be hard on" or "Don't stir up anger in your children." So, basically, all of this can be done in a right way—not some kind of power trip, not discouraging them, but having a plan and lovingly following through with it. Mom, you are off the hook on this one. Well, not exactly, but it's interesting how God knows human nature, and while not always, often it does seem like the harshness comes more from dads, and that's probably why God said it just like He did.

There are many other Scriptures we could use, and we will prepare the soil a bit more in the next chapter, but the bottom line here is we're not just throwing some old-timey thing on you. God said it is very important.

IMPORTANT BUT WHY?

Why would this obedience issue be so important in this first Spring Season of parenting? God always has good reasons for why He says things, so let's think this through a minute. Little kids naturally want to be in control (it's the "be like God" thing). That sinful nature that all of us are born with doesn't want to submit to authority, so every child has to be trained from a very young age that they are under your authority. God places you as a parent in your child's life to bring discipline and authority into their lives, much as God is the authority in our lives as adults.

Since God puts you as the authority over your little child, you should embrace that. It may be good to say this a few times: "I am in control over my child." This is the truth, and you should own and believe it. You actually do have control over them; the biggest challenge actually is whether you will take it. For me (Deb) as a mom, I used to actually tell myself over and over that I am in charge, not the child. It gets so easy to just let the kids lead and do what they want. It seems easier a lot of the time and we as moms get tired and worn down. So, if you have to tell yourself five times in a row, go ahead and do it! I did, it went like this, "I am in charge, I am in charge, I am in charge of this child. He is not the boss of me, I am in charge of him!"

Let me tell you a difficult truth. If your little children do not obey you, guess where the blame lies? Now we're starting to meddle, aren't we? *God has given you* control over your little children. And this is the specific season to do it in, when you actually *do have* control. If your three-year-old defies you, or rather *when* she defies you, you have the responsibility and authority to control that behavior and bring loving discipline. We were just talking with our daughter-in-law the other day. She had been having challenges with her little 2-year-old and she said the thing that made the most difference was for her to remember, "I'm in control here" not my little guy, and take it back. The time to begin giving away your authority to your child will come—in the Fall Season, which ironically, you often *won't* feel like doing then. But not now! Don't give away your authority in your little child's life. In this season, you are their parent, not their friend. Not now. This is critical.

If you embrace this, then your child will be happier and ready for that next Summer Season of *Teaching* and *Vision*. Too often we ignore this during this Spring Season time because we don't really think it's a big deal. I mean, how much damage can a little cute 20-pound person really do, right? Or you don't believe it's important because you are concerned you'll stifle their "self-expression" or you are spending all your time trying to win the prize for "youngest kid to read" award. What can easily happen is that you miss the most important thing—*Obedience* and *Heart*—then, when that next Summer Season comes around, they are entitled and truly believe they are the center of the universe. They think they know more than mom and dad, so they start to challenge you with everything you say.

Think of it this way. By prioritizing obedience and discipline young, you are giving your child the invaluable *gift* of self-discipline. And that is such an important quality to gain for all of the following seasons. Here is the part that is not obvious. Self-discipline doesn't come from ourselves; it is given by others. Well-known psychologists Drs. Henry Cloud and John Townsend say in their excellent book *How People Grow*:

> Self-discipline is always a fruit of 'other' discipline. Some people get disciplined by other people early in life and then internalize it into their character, then they possess it themselves. Other people don't get disciplined early in life and they don't ever have self-discipline until they get it from others and internalize it for themselves. (Pg 125)

If you as their parent, don't prioritize this during the first Spring Season, then they won't have self-discipline internalized for themselves. Then it will be left up to teachers and coaches to try to instill in the next season, bosses in the next, and sadly sometimes judges and prison wardens in the next. Each season later, it gets *more challenging* with *greater consequences.*

Now is the time! This is why during this first season, by you taking your responsibility to lovingly enforce discipline, you are transferring into their heart and character the *gift of self-discipline* which sets them up so wonderfully to receive the *Teaching* and *Vision* that are the main focuses to be cultivated into their lives in the Summer Season (7-12). I hope you pause and consider the impact of this. If you miss this now, it has to come from somewhere—but all of the sources that bring this discipline later are more disruptive and impede the actual growth and fruit that you desire to see in the next seasons. Each season builds upon the prior. If everything is prioritized and focused on in the right time, then the best opportunity exists for the following seasons to unfold with maximum positive effect . . . and peace!

HEART PEACE

So, relax and don't worry that your child will get behind if they are not the first one to join in every reindeer game; dance, little-league, pre pre pre pre school academics, etc. Let everybody else win the prize for that stuff. Sadly, often so many *activities* become the focus during this first season. It's so cute to see little kiddos on the soccer field running the wrong direction and dancing with funny childish moves. Some of this is fine, but if we get engrossed with all these activities *and forget the most important things* we should be focusing on, training them to obey and have a sweet, happy heart, we miss the main point and focus at a critical time.

They get all these accolades for being the smartest, best dancer, best sports whatever, and it reinforces the false notion that they are little gods and are in control. Don't forget—we are talking children 0-6 here. There is plenty of time for this attention, but during this season, focus on getting your little kids to obey you in everything with a genuinely happy, contented attitude. That too is possible— it's the heart piece (funny, I accidentally typed heart "peace") but that is actually pretty accurate. When you focus on making the number one priority in their little lives' obedience with the right attitude, it produces heart peace. You will have a happy and much more contented child.

Now of course, they don't realize this. Their little flesh wants to defy you, be in control, get what they want, then change what they want, and run you around like crazy mom. But they still won't be happy, and you certainly won't be! Ironically, the more freedom they are given during this young season, the less happy and content they are. I'm going to say that again. The more freedom they are given during this young season, *the less happy and content they are.* What they *really want* is to have you be in control. That's the way God designed it; to live in an environment where there are clear boundaries and clear and predictable consequences when they break them. That is what produces secure, happy, confident children that are ready to learn and grow better and faster than ever when summer starts. It's not as hard as it might sound with focus and intentionality.

HUMAN LABORATORY

Deb and I have five kids, and when they were young, I had this theory regarding the importance of obedience and heart when they were little, so that is basically all we focused on (plus the things in the upcoming "Always in Season" chapter). The theory went something like this, "We are going to focus on *Obedience* and *Heart* when they are little, and we are not going to be busy getting involved in academics or too many extras, and if they are healthy and happy now, they will be able to easily learn more difficult subjects later on with far less stress."

Now, we homeschooled our kids, so this afforded us more flexibility and control over their academic progress. And so, when they were little, that was the main thing—play and obey. We were in no hurry to have them jump into tense academics. We saw many people stressing and trying to get their kids to learn more and more, sooner and sooner, and we just left our kids be kids; we played a lot and taught household chores—we expected obedience with a right heart, but that was about it. Then, when they were 16 . . . just kidding, but we didn't focus too much on academics until they were about seven, and even then, we kept working on heart and obedience things.

Every year they would take the standardized tests and so far, my theory was right on. Most of them were behind academically. We stressed out a little bit over that, but they were happy, obedient, energetic, and interested kids. What if the next part of the theory didn't work, the part where they were supposed to soar on ahead as they got older and could learn things like the three "R's" quickly and stress-free as their minds and emotions were more developed? Then we would be in trouble.

We continued taking those standardized tests and they were almost always behind in most subjects. A couple times, they were as far as three years behind. It wasn't something we bragged about, but nevertheless, that's what was happening. We focused on one main thing—obedience in everything, and the right heart attitude behind it, plus having a lot of fun. So, when we said, "Kid's get your shoes, it's time to leave." They just did it because we expected it and it had become normal to them. They were now internalizing self-discipline, and it was quickly becoming their own. It was really a peaceful way to live, and they were content and happy children because our boundaries and expectations were clear.

But then an interesting thing happened. Somewhere around 3rd, 4th, 5th grade, and into middle school, they just started catching up and excelling. They learned concepts quickly and relatively easily. The theory was that if they had their own built-in discipline, and confidence that obedience in a loving atmosphere brought, minus the entire stress high academic and extracurricular pressure puts on young kids, they would much more quickly grasp concepts. And in the end, it worked out.

They easily caught up and when they were juniors in high school, all of them enrolled in community college as dual enrolled students where college credits counted both for college and high school; so now they were making double-time. Their entire junior and senior years were completed in community college, gaining both high school and college credit. Two of them actually graduated from high school with associates degrees, and the others all had enough credits transfer into their bachelors' program to cut off at least a year. Today, four out of the five have bachelor's degrees, and one of those went on to get a masters. This is not to imply college is the end-all in importance. Education may be facing a change like the horse and buggy companies did after Henry Ford came along. It is just to say at least the slow academic start *didn't* hamper their learning.

EVERYTHING IN SEASON

The whole point of this book is everything in the proper season. Parenting is such a long, slow process and it can be very confusing with so many ideas floating around but if you get the right focus at the right time, that will give you the best opportunity to enjoy the next season. Years ago, I saw this Influence and Power Graph somewhere, and I cannot remember or find where it was—so, this is not original, and whoever came up with this, thank you.

Influence/power graph.

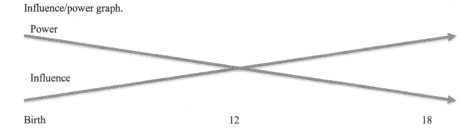

The above graph is helpful to recognize why taking your God-given responsibility seriously to enforce obedience when your children are young is so important. On the top left of the graph is "power." When your children are young, you have complete power over them. You feed them. You change them. You provide absolutely everything for them. So, the statement I encouraged you to repeat earlier is *true*, "I am in control over my child." On the bottom left of the graph is "influence." That is simply the respect and place you have earned in their lives that makes them desire and *want* to model after you or listen to your advice. Again, when they are little, you have none of that because you are just starting out.

Over time, a very interesting thing happens. As they grow older, transitioning from spring to summer, around age seven, you have less power over them than when they were two. Hopefully, your influence is growing. Transitioning from summer to fall, around 12-13 right in the middle of the graph, you have much less power yet; and they enjoy demonstrating that. You'll notice at this time, the two lines cross. Then, over to the right-hand side, when your child is 18 and beyond, you have basically no power over them, and *all you have left is your influence.*

Sadly, many parents can get this completely backwards. They try to be their little child's friend, treating them like peers and giving them all sorts of choices. What do you want to eat? What do you want to wear? Do you want this or that? And you let the little guy run you around while you simply try to be nice and exert "influence." Then, at 14 and 15, when they are doing some serious damage, the parent comes in with the power and tries to bring down the hammer. Now the parent is shouting something like, "I am in control here, listen to me!" But sadly, it is no longer true. You let the child control you when they were younger, so they know you *were never* in control, and you are definitely not in control now when they know *everything* as a teenager! It was true that you did have control—in the first season, but it's not true in the Fall Harvest Season. You may have a little power over them, but it is usually far less than you realize. All you end up with is your influence. Think about this carefully.

Ironically, the very thing you often "feel" like doing in any given season, is the opposite of what you should do. When they are young, you may feel like you want to let them have their own way, be their friend, give them freedom. But the opposite is true then. However, when they are teenagers, you will "feel" like grounding, stamping, hounding and clamping—all power stuff. But, ironically, the right thing to do now is release, more and more. It's now harvest time, and oh it comes so quickly! Don't ignore any of these seasons, for unlike farming, you only go through each one once in parenting.

MIXING SEASONS

We as parents often do things in the wrong season but once you recognize this concept of the four seasons, it can be liberating and even transform your parenting! However, as you are living through it one day at a time, it is not intuitive or obvious. In fact, about the time you recognize that "Whoa, something needs to be done here!" Often, one or even two seasons have passed.

Let me illustrate. In this section, the *Spring Planting: Heart and Obedience Season* from about 1-6yrs, this is the time specifically where those little children that God has given you are to be brought into complete obedience while training their heart as we've discussed. When the Bible says, "Children, obey your parents in everything" it's not talking about 25-year-olds—those are adults. It is important in this season for that little will to be brought into complete obedience. But it's not obvious, and it's even funny at times when they are defiant. And so, with many things going on in life, we often don't really take the time to focus on the importance of bringing that little will into subjection to their God-given authority (that's *you*).

We may just let their stubbornness and defiance pass through the Spring Season and that little "plant" keeps growing right along with their stubborn insubordinate will. If you didn't get their will brought into obedience in the first season, there is still time in the Summer Season, but it is much more difficult and less effective—but certainly still worthwhile and impacting. But again, if parents didn't think about it or value it in the first season when the child was young, they often are just busy and going through life in the Summer Season of parenting from ages 7-12 as well.

Then, in the Fall Harvest Season—the teenage years—the fruit is now coming out and maturing. Now as parents, we are sitting up and taking notice! This "child" is now big and hairy and his defiant attitude and actions can really cause some problems. At that point you may yell, "You better listen to me!!!" Then the son looks down at mom and in his deepening voice laughs, ignores, mocks, or worse. It's the same will at four years old when they look at you and defy you as 14, or put another way 15 pounds as 150 pounds. The difference is at 15 pounds, you had complete ability to control the child—whether you take it or not, is what this book is about. At 150 pounds, you have very little actual power (sometimes we are the last to realize that)—what you are left with is your influence.

I once talked with a mom that was complaining to me that she ran around chasing her 150-pound son to discipline him, trying to spank him. At this point he was eating sandwiches bigger than she was. It was the right thing—but the wrong season. That season had passed. The more you try to enforce discipline in this Fall Harvest Season, the more it can cause rebellion—the total opposite effect we desire. The reason is that sadly, this is now two seasons past the ideal time to be focusing on their obedience and discipline. It's the right thing at the wrong time; much like planting corn in the fall. In many instances at this point, rather than try to clamp down and enforce obedience, it is better to relax, because fall is the Encouragement and Releasing Season.

CHOICES CHOICES

One reason this can be so difficult to see is that most of these activities are right things—the variable is *when* they are to be done.

Let me give you one more example: giving your child choices. So often parents naturally think they want to give their little children choices so that they grow up being able to make decisions and be an independent person—and that is very true, if done at the right time.

In the Spring Heart and Obedience Season—approximately birth – six, they should be given very few choices, and when they are given, they are the exception and not the rule. On the surface, that perhaps seems extreme or like they will grow up being repressed and unable to make decisions or be responsible. This concern is understandable because when your child is 18 you really do want them to be able to make good choices because at that time, they will really be making nearly all of their choices. Because of this confusion, we allow the children freedom of choice and lack of discipline too young. The result of this is that it causes them to become *insecure and lacking self-control* later. It's not intuitive— applying discipline and not allowing choices in the Spring Season produces self-discipline and confidence to make better choices later.

Often, we are afraid to discipline and be their authority, so we give our little 5-year-old all kinds of choices and we try to reason with them, so they feel "respected" or have "self-expression." Then when our 15-year-old has no discipline and thinks they run the universe, we ground and remove all of their choices. That is the time you really want them to be making good choices—because in just a few years, whether we like it or not, they are making all of their choices as we watch on.

So, you can see, getting the right thing in the right season is crucial, but mixing the seasons is what we can naturally tend to do. Let me (Deb) give you a very tangible example of how this works in the area of food and meals first. Mommy tells the children they are having scrambled eggs for breakfast. Little Johnny says "I don't like scrambled eggs, I want cereal." Mom says, "Well Johnny, Mommy has decided we are all having scrambled eggs today." Everyone sits down to eat their terrible plate of eggs and Johnny fusses and refuses to eat. No reason for mom to get exasperated or upset because of his behavior, she clearly knows *she is in control* and has an intentional plan. She doesn't try to force him to eat and when everyone else is finished eating, Mom simply tells Johnny that if he gets hungry and wants something to eat before lunch, he will have to eat his scrambled eggs. When his little sister gets a morning snack (which you make sure to give her that morning) Johnny doesn't get one. His only choice is to eat his scrambled eggs that are left over from breakfast—yum!

What this does is teaches Johnny that Mom is in charge and that there are no other choices. When lunchtime comes, it is remarkable how much more willing little Johnny is to eat whatever Mommy makes because he is very hungry. At this point, the scrambled eggs can be offered to Fluffy.

It's so simple and peaceful when Mom has a plan and is in charge of most of the decisions—when the little children are given choices, it is an exception; considered a privilege not a right. Of course, she knows her children and their preferences and chooses their favorite foods often. But at times she wants to stretch them to try new things and test their obedience as well.

If Mom doesn't understand this principle that her children need to know that she is the authority, then the example would go more like this: Mommy tells the children we are having scrambled eggs for breakfast. Little Johnny complains and says, "I don't like scrambled eggs, I want cereal." Mommy tries to coax him to want scrambled eggs. Little Suzie hears the discussion and says she now wants pancakes. At this point, Mom is starting to feel frustration and getting a bit angry that breakfast is getting so difficult. "Why can't these kids just listen to me!?" About this time Johnny whines, "I want Lucky Charms." Now Mom might give in and say, "OK, you can have Lucky Charms" and then still make scrambled eggs, but now Suzie is upset because she didn't get pancakes!

Or Mom can proceed to become a gourmet chef and make everything to each child's changing preferences and now she's feeling angry and like things are backwards, because they are! The kids are the authority and Mom follows their orders. This will continue with most choices until *Mom stops it*! Children will always try to get their way. I have not met one self-less child. We all come into this world wanting our own way.

It's our job as parents to teach the children what submission is all about so as they grow up and walk with Jesus, they will more naturally be able to follow what the Word says and walk a godly lifestyle even when they don't really feel like it or want to do it. You have given them the *priceless gift* of learning to submit their will at a young age. Your discipline now gives them the gift of self-discipline later.

We have literally seen a child fuss and complain that they did not like the cheeseburger that was made at a family cookout. The parent sympathized with the child and said, "Do you want me to run to McDonald's and get you a cheeseburger baby?" And the parent literally left the party, went to McDonald's and got their kid a "Happy Meal" while everyone else ate those terrible home grilled burgers! Besides *not* being happy, this teaches the child a couple things: 1) They are in charge. 2) Daddy and Mommy are on this planet to serve my every wish. Repeat this over and over, every day and you are producing an entitled unhappy child, a frazzled parent, and a chaotic environment. Learn and apply the concepts of seasons of parenting and you and your children will experience greater peace.

QUESTIONS FOR DISCUSSION

1. What is the top priority to train for in this season? Discuss this and why it is important.

2. Whose responsibility is it to apply the verses regarding children obeying parents?

3. Why is it a temptation to get ahead of yourself, doing too many things too early and what would be the reason to take your time and just concentrate on the main thing in each season? Discuss examples of that.

4. Why is it important to remind yourself that you actually are in charge of your child? How does that help? Discuss examples.

5. Discuss the promise and the warning in Ephesians 6:1-4.

6. Reread the quote from "How People Grow" on page 20. How do kids gain self-discipline? Discuss how this gets more difficult with greater consequences when not prioritized in this first season.

7. Look at the "Influence/Power" chart on page 24 and discuss what that means to you. How does that inform the importance of discipline and obedience in this first season compared to later?

SEASONS OF PARENTING

CHAPTER 2

HOW AND WHEN TO DISCIPLINE

The subject of discipline, and particularly "spanking" has become very unpopular. One reason is because it has become misused involving anger and random application which can be abuse. Biblical spanking never involves anger and has a specific plan. The two are not even distant relatives. Understanding the difference clears up a lot of confusion and brings confidence to parents and happiness and peace to children.

Discipline is only used once you have spent adequate time training. Setting up training sessions *is key* to raising happy healthy obedient children and is the *most important part* of disciplining.

Many parents skip this step of training which unfortunately puts the child at such a disadvantage because they don't even know what the parent expects. Let's look at this extended passage to get God's perspective on discipline:

> My son, do not make light of the Lord's discipline, and do not lose heart when he rebukes you, because the Lord disciplines those he loves, and he punishes everyone he accepts as a son. Endure hardship as discipline; God is treating you as sons. For what son is not disciplined by his father? If you are not disciplined (and everyone undergoes discipline) then you are illegitimate children and not true sons. Moreover, we have all had human fathers who disciplined us and we respected them for it . . . No discipline seems pleasant at the time, but painful. Later on however, it produces a harvest of righteousness and peace for those who have been trained by it.
> Hebrews 12:5-11 (portions)

This passage highlights the fact that we train and discipline *because* we love our children. The two are directly connected, and sadly, sometimes in our culture it can seem like love and discipline are viewed as opposites. They are not—discipline, done in the right manner, is love.

BIBLICAL FOUNDATION

We are very aware that this subject has become hotly debated and many people today reject this all together; you may find yourself there right now, or wrestling with it. The following verses have provided a strong biblical foundation for spanking and helped me

(Deb) stick with the concept because I too would have rather not spanked. It is easier to let it go and just ignore the behavior or just talk and reason with them. But talking and reasoning is a great example of the right thing at the wrong time—that comes in the next season. I decided that I was going to go to the Bible and use it as my guide in how to discipline my children. I believe God's Word always has the answers above my own thoughts and wishes. Look at these examples:

> Do not withhold discipline from a child; if you strike him with a rod, he will not die. Proverbs 23:13 (ESV)

Notice here, discipline and striking with a rod are the same thing—striking with a rod is discipline, even though it *feels* offensive to so many people.

> If you strike him with the rod, you will deliver him from death. Proverbs 23:14 (NET Bible)

> Foolishness is bound up in the heart of a child, but the rod of discipline drives it far from him.
> Proverbs 22:15 (Berean Standard Bible)

Here, the rod is the instrument that delivers from death and drives out foolishness. If I asked any parent, "Do you want your child delivered from death and foolishness?" Every parent would say, "Absolutely!" But here, the rod—used in striking—is the very means of this deliverance! We desire the outcome, but many reject the means to the outcome.

One young couple took this to heart and were very intentional on training sessions and discipline, and it literally saved their son from death. Remember, the training sessions that we will describe shortly, go hand in hand. Once he was trained, one time he was running out onto the road into oncoming traffic, and they said "stop" and he just listened—it saved his life; it literally delivered him from death. They utilized training sessions with spanking consistently and their boys learned quickly.

> The rod and reproof give wisdom, but a child left to himself brings shame to his mother. Proverbs 29:15 (ESV)

The rod in this instance imparts wisdom. By applying corporal punishment at the right time and in the right manner, the natural foolishness that is in a child is driven out and wisdom is brought in. That is one trade you definitely want to make.

> Discipline your son, and he will give you rest; he will bring delight to your soul. Proverbs 29:17 (Berean Standard Bible)

This same couple took seriously the next section on training sessions. They took the time to train their boys what the word "no" and "stop" meant and how to obey when they said those words. They applied small swats to reinforce the concept of "No, don't touch that" and the boys quickly learned not to touch when they heard the word "no." These parents gave their boys a great gift of self-discipline at a young age.

They have twins and on their first Christmas, they were 11 months old. Because they applied training and discipline early, the boys left the Christmas tree ornaments alone. Most people would think that's too young or not possible, but they diligently took it to heart and did it. They said, now that their boys are five, they almost never have to use the paddle because they are so obedient, and they have incredible peace and rest because of it. "Discipline your son, and he will give you rest." And it's probably more important than ever if you have twins!

"Whoever spares the rod hates their children, but the one who loves their children is careful to discipline them." Proverbs 13:24

That last verse is probably the most shocking and offensive of all of them: If you skip spanking you hate your children! Wow—talk about the exact opposite of what our culture is peddling! If we want to live our lives according to the Bible, we cannot ignore these verses on how to train our children. So many fads come and go. I believe the Bible has answers to most of our daily life questions, if we are open and willing to submit ourselves to follow them. I know it is hard to do something you don't want to do, but that is what Jesus did for us. He is our example.

The Bible speaks of a rod. I spent time fighting this idea too, read articles and books about it, but I could not come up with something to fight against the Scripture. God's Word is full of wisdom. If we just use our hand—which is always available, that can cause the child to flinch at a sudden movement or allow us to be reactive. So, God's Word says to use a different instrument for discipline and allow our hands to be used for helping and affection.

I made a conscious decision to embrace what the Bible says to use and I went to the store and bought a dowel rod. A hardware store will usually have a section with all sizes. I bought one of the smallest ones and cut it into three pieces. This became my spanking or training instrument for the training sessions. As the kids got bigger, we used a wooden paddle when we spanked them on their bottoms as we will describe shortly.

TRAINING SESSIONS

An easy example for all parents to understand is training the child what the word "no" means. Before the child is one, he can be trained to respond to a calm gentle "no." Here is how you do it. Set the child (around 10 months) on your lap and put something colorful and tempting for him to touch. As he reaches out to touch it gently say "No." If he continues to reach for it swat the top of his hand lightly with the dowel rod while saying "No." He will pull his hand away and look at you and wonder what just happened. Most likely he will try again within a minute, and you follow the same steps. It usually only takes a few times of going through this training to teach him the word "No." Congratulations you have gained a great victory already before your child is one!

The reason for swatting the hand while saying "No" is so the child associates an unpleasant feeling enough to stop what he is doing when he hears "no." I once was at a friend's house and their child was in a walker and scooted to where mommy had plants growing and was pulling off leaves and eating them. Her mommy scolded her and said "No! Don't eat the plants." I was thinking if mommy would have taken the time to go over to the baby and swatted her hand while she said no, the baby would stop. But the baby continued to pull leaves off and was eating them. I suppose plant-based diets are healthy, but finally mommy was highly frustrated and started raising her voice, which is what happens when you do not have a plan and have not gone through training sessions. If mommy would have inflicted just a tiny bit of pain with the word "no," it would have been an unpleasant experience for the baby, and she would have stopped. The two need to go together.

By setting up training sessions like this you are setting up who is in control and who is the authority. When he pulls on your earrings or glasses you have already trained him to respond to the word no, so all you have to do is gently say no. And he will not continue to pull on your earrings or glasses or eat all your plants.

ADVANCING TRAINING SESSIONS

As the child grows so do the training sessions. Anything that is important to you as parents, you can teach and train the child to respond the way you want him to. You as the parents just have to think about it and come up with a priority list of what you care most about and train for it. If you make your goal being 100% consistent with the small type of discipline while training, they will learn.

As they get older, between two and three, it is important to sit them down and in great detail explain to them what you are wanting to teach them. Make out your plan about what you want to work on, how you plan to do it, and what type of discipline you will use if they do not follow your steps. By this time, we are transitioning from the dowel rod to a wooden paddle and begin discipline with spankings, as we'll explain shortly.

For example, every child around 1-year-old needs to be trained to "come here." Tell the child, "When mommy says to come here, I want you to come. If you don't come, you will get a swat on your hand with a dowel rod." Then start practice sessions. Set the child down 10 feet away and tell them to come. If they come, you pick them up and celebrate. If they refuse, then you go and swat their hand, and try it again. Most of the time, after three times of doing this consistently, children get it. Then you can practice doing that several times in the same day to establish this.

The next morning, you remind them and practice it at least 10 times during the second day. By the end of that day, they will be trained. The challenge is that you have to continue to pay attention to what you are training and saying, and when they disobey, you provide the discipline consistently. The same would apply for telling mommy "No," not opening the refrigerator door, not going into the pantry, whining and begging for something after mom said no, asking twice once mom said no, interrupting, and 100 other examples you encounter.

One way to stay focused was that I would mark off 2-3 days on the calendar and did not plan to accomplish much else besides what I had decided to train for. That became my main priority for those few days. I would explain in great detail my plan and then we would have a practice day. I would remind often throughout the first day what we are working on and the plan of how to get the desired outcome and it was usually a pleasant day of practicing the new thing. The child is not in trouble, just in training.

The next day I would go over it again in the morning and tell them now today the discipline will be added when they do not do it right. It was my focus for the day to train myself and them of what we were working on. By the end of the 2nd day the child usually has been trained, if mommy was consistent (this is the main key to success). It is mommy that has to implement these training sessions and see that they happen and continue to keep the standard the same. Really, the biggest challenge is for *us as parents* to see the need and stay focused on it.

DISCIPLINE

Using an instrument to discipline your child is a topic that is tough to talk about. I hope you hear me on this because my bent (Deb) is to *love, love, love*. Spanking is not a fun thing for me. Literally sometimes when one of my children needed a spanking, I'd go in my room and talk to the Lord and cry, saying, "Lord, I don't want to spank him. Please help me to do this." It is not something that I took pleasure in. I cannot recall a time I spanked my children while angry. Please listen to this next sentence:

If you are angry at your child, DO NOT spank them.

If you set up the training sessions like I mentioned earlier and follow your steps, you never have to get angry because you have a pre-thought-out plan and you simply follow the steps. Emotions are not elevated. There is no anger. Actually, it is having a discipline plan that *removes* the anger and brings peace. Honestly, as I write this, tears are coming to my eyes as I remember back how hard it was for me in the days of spanking. I really did not like the idea of inflicting pain on my cute little precious kid, but I had studied and researched and found in Scriptures that the Bible had a very clear plan on how to raise children. It was my choice whether to follow the Bible's prescribed plan or not. I chose to deny my wishes and preferences and do what the Bible taught. I hope you will too.

When parents do not have a plan and just start swinging or hitting when anger or emotions are high, that is when abuse can happen. What we are describing here has nothing at all to do with this. In fact, if you take these principles and methods to heart, it will produce the exact opposite. This is why the subject can get heated, complicated, or confusing. Those two can sound similar, because perhaps an instrument is used, but they are not even distant relatives. What we are teaching here is a planned, controlled method of using the biblical rod for the purpose of training your young children. Remember, this is the Spring Season ages 0-6, and done properly, spanking is pretty much over by then as your children have been trained in obedience.

DETAILS OF HOW TO DISCIPLINE

Explain your expectations and work on one issue at a time. Don't overwhelm the child and yourself with focusing on too many things. Pay close attention to what you are telling them to do. *Watch* to see if they obey and listen. If they do not obey, go to them right away and say in a calm, caring voice, "Oh, you did not obey mommy, now we have to go get a spanking." Notice here that this is done in a controlled manner. There is no out of control tempers going on— mom is not yelling or even angry. More so, the spanking is done in sorrow and out of obedience to the Word. Here are some suggested steps for spanking that will help everything to progress in a calm and controlled way:

- If a child will walk, take the child away from all others (if not you will have to carry him). Spanking and correcting in a private place is respectful to the child. It is degrading to spank a child in front of other friends, adults, or siblings.

- Tell them what your expectations were and how you had already talked the plan over with them and remind them what they did wrong.

- Have the child lay on their stomach on a bed if available; this is to help them learn to submit themselves. Also, going to a different room helps to prevent reactive discipline and keeps it from embarrassing the child. Go through the steps with the child you are going to use to spank them.

- Tell them to lay still and do not put their hands back on their bottom, or you will accidently hit their hands.

- Spank them with a wooden paddle, not a belt or anything flimsy. It's more difficult to aim with a belt; you do not know where the belt will land. The Bible said use a rod, not a whip. We are 100% careful to administer the spanking to the buttocks. Make sure to hit the chubby part of their bottoms (you don't want to hit their back or their legs) The number of spankings depends on what was done; usually 1, 2 or 3, never more.

- Let the child cry for two to three minutes but do not allow screaming. Screaming displays defiance and rebellion, crying displays sorrow.

- Take the child on your lap while they cry and hold them and talk about what they did to get the spanking. Particularly, if they do scream or start swinging their limbs, hold them on your lap and hold their arms tight like a firm hug and talk to them about how to control our arms and hands.

- Role play (verbally) what they did and what they should have done.

- Explain in great detail how you want them to handle this same situation the next time.

- Tell them that you love them, that is *why* you are taking the time to train them and teach them.

- Hold them for a few more minutes, give hugs and reassure of your love.

If spanking is done properly, most children will be trained by age seven, ironically, the first year of summer! Rarely will you need to spank past that. So put another way—spanking is primarily for the Spring Season.

A SIMPLE EXAMPLE

A mommy called me one day asking for help. Her 2-year-old toddler kept going into the bathroom and pulling the toilet paper off the roll and emptying some of the drawers. He was starting to do these many times a day. Mommy was starting to get really frustrated.

I suggested putting a line of duct tape on the floor across the doorway and telling her toddler if he crossed the line, he would get a spanking. He was not allowed to go over this line. I encouraged her to spend one day practicing and the next day adding the spanking if he crossed the duct tape. She was willing to try it. She called back after two days and said it was a *miracle*! It worked! He was consistently staying out of the bathroom and never crossing the line. We just have to be smarter than they are. When we use the Bible for our instructions, the results will be amazing.

We recently had a young couple call us and want to go out to dinner and talk about how they can get their little guy to listen to them. We have talked with them through the years and have watched their little fellow grow to where today he is five. In the past, they had applied the discipline of spanking, but then it gets confusing with so much other contrary information. Others had said not to spank, so they stopped and were taking things away, having him sit in a corner staring at the wall, and grounding and removing privileges sometimes for days. These types of things have increased chaos in their home and disobedience has gotten out of hand.

As we talked about it, we just encouraged them to go back to God's Word. God says the rod of discipline will drive out folly. We suggested they sit their child down and talk to him about how he has started to be extremely disobedient, and Mommy and Daddy want to follow what the Bible says. It says when your children disobey, they should get a spanking. So, we are going to start doing this. Explain with details and examples, even role-playing what you mean. Then say, "Tomorrow we will start to practice obeying." Have a practice day then the next day add spanking when the child chooses to disobey. Remember to always show love after the spanking by hugging, holding them, and playing. Make sure they know the slate has been wiped clean. Nothing is carried over to a later time or day. The offense got taken care of immediately, now we move forward.

We talked with this young couple a few weeks later and they were so much happier and so was the child. Things had changed in the home almost miraculously and immediately, by simplifying the process and applying the biblical discipline lovingly and quickly, settling it now and then moving on.

TEMPER TANTRUMS

Throughout the Spring Season, you need to continue to remind yourself that you are in control and say what you mean and mean what you say. In most cases a child will try to use temper tantrums to get their way. But if properly dealt with, the tantrum will not get the desired result so the child will not try it very long. In case you aren't familiar with tantrums, the root cause of tantrums is that the child did not get his way, so he is exercising everything he has to show his will and his defiance by throwing himself down, hitting, screaming and flailing around like a fish out of water. This is simply the most dramatic and defiant manner in which they can exert their little will.

They are doing this because of something you are wanting them to do or not do that they disagree with. It is essential to recognize this. While it can be dramatic, alarming, and disruptive the basic element is the same: disobedience. Your will against their will. We've read "experts" who say you should just let it happen, ignore it, and try not to be embarrassed if this is at the grocery store or at a park. One psychologist said to try not making eye contact with people who are around while your child is having the tantrum, even if it lasts 15 minutes. Also, the same article said if the child continues the tantrums, you should seek medical advice from your doctor or psychologist. When I heard this, I really wondered if this psychologist has any children. Most children will try this, it is not unusual. It is not a "medical" condition that a doctor needs to help with. It is simply a little child wanting his own way. And this is the only way he knows how to show it. Parent, you need to be loving but little junior needs to know that you are the authority, not him. It is time to show him.

We would suggest treating it the same as any other disobedience. Take the child that is defying you by choosing to have a tantrum and tell them, "Mommy is in charge here and I can see that you are upset and do not like what I said, but this is the way it is, and I am not changing my mind. You can choose to act this way, or you can decide to control yourself and tell me how you are feeling. But Mommy is not changing my mind."

If he chooses to continue having the tantrum, the two most effective things to do are, either remove him from everyone so that he does not have anyone for an audience. If no one is watching, they usually will not continue thrashing around, kicking or screaming. It's not nearly as interesting if no one is watching. Or you can tell him if he chooses to continue having the tantrum you are going to give him a spanking. After the spanking, hold him, give him attention and reassure of your love, talking about how you want him to act the next time. If he will not quit crying or continues to scream, take him to a different room and tell him he can come out when he chooses to be happy.

This whole process is so important for you to teach him because he needs to learn how to control his will and emotions now. If you just sit back and watch like the psychologist mentioned earlier, we will have 1st graders throwing themselves on the ground, kicking and screaming when the teacher tells them to do things that they don't want to do. How is this supposed to work in classroom settings?

Or when they get older and have jobs and their boss tells them to do something they do not want to do, they will throw themselves on the ground and start kicking and screaming—maybe not, but they will walk out in a hissy-fit. Someone just told me yesterday about how a kid quit the little league team. The coach had told him he needed to do something, and he didn't like it, so the kid said he was going to quit at the end of the game, perhaps thinking that threat would cause the coach to back down. The coach said, "Where are your parents, we'll just take care of this now." And the boy was done.

We all have to learn to submit our wills to somebody someday. Submitting to authority is a valuable lesson we are to teach our children, and *particularly* in this Spring Season.

A WORD ON GROUNDING

It is interesting, while spanking has become unpopular, the idea of grounding doesn't seem to get much scrutiny. The term was initially used in aviation. When a pilot was prevented from flying an aircraft due to misconduct, illness, or technical issues the pilot was "grounded" or literally confined to the ground.

We think grounding is best left to be used for pilots. I can't think of one time we ever grounded our kids, and yet we constantly hear of parents grounding their kids for all kinds of things. For little kids, it's confusing. The idea of dragging punishments out over an extended time of hours or days for a young child isn't helpful and is actually very confusing. If you separate the consequence from the offense, in their little mind it gets all muddled and disjointed. They become insecure and confused, not even remembering why they haven't been able to leave their room for three days. The discipline and training need to be closely tied to the offense.

For teenagers it becomes a seedbed for bitterness to internally take root over the days of consequence during a season for releasing. Grounding is applying power at a time when influence is mostly what you have from the prior graph. They may stay confined for a time, but often the earliest possible opportunity they have to leave, they will be gone.

The goal of this chapter was to describe training sessions and types of discipline, and particularly spanking, giving the biblical support as well as very practical application on how and when to apply it helping you to have the ability to bring obedience to this formative Spring Season.

QUESTIONS FOR DISCUSSION

1. Discuss training sessions and write out one that you want to do with your child. Why are these training sessions important?

2. Explain and discuss taking a day just for training. How does the phrase, "The child is not in trouble, just in training" change your view on discipline?

3. Relook at Hebrews 12:5-11 and discuss what you learn there about discipline.

4. Discuss the Bible verses about spanking; what is the most difficult? What are the most surprising connections these verses make between spanking and your child's life?

5. How would having a pre-thought plan of discipline help us as parents with our emotions?

6. Should we or should we not ever spank when we are angry at our child? Discuss the difference in the two.

7. What is the root of a temper-tantrum and what are the two best ways to deal with it? Which one would you lean towards and why?

CHAPTER 3

TIPS TO STAY FOCUSED

The training, discipline, and obedience described in the prior chapters may seem challenging, but we want to encourage you, it is doable! Probably the biggest challenge that we have seen through the years is parents believing that their child is the exception to the rules. For some reason, it may work on every other child, but not theirs.

MY CHILD'S THE EXCEPTION

We have heard over and over, "I've tried discipline. We've spanked and spanked. It doesn't work." There are usually some creative reasons why their particular child is the exception. Here is the truth, the vast majority of the time it's our problem *as parents*. I know, I hate it when that happens. The real issue is parents *being consistent; paying attention; staying at it*. It takes intentionality to have training sessions, follow through, be consistent. But I can't think of anything more worthwhile.

And it's interesting, those little kids seem to have nothing to do all day but think of ways to find a loophole. So, this chapter is going to be dedicated to helping you find ways so that your child can be brought into complete obedience during this first Spring Season. We don't want you to miss tackling this now, because this is the season for training for obedience.

Children from 1-6 are pliable and moldable much like a tender young plant. You can bend it where you want it to go with just a little pressure. It was interesting when I used to farm, in spring, just after the corn came up, you could even drive a tractor over a little corn stock and it would pop back up, but wait until the summer and do that, and it breaks off. A little oak tree that has just sprouted up from an acorn can also be bent over and popped back up—do it a little later and you will break it—a little later yet and there is no more bending at all! Don't wait until the next season. It will be much harder.

NEW EVERY MORNING

A huge hurdle is that this first season of six years lasts over 2,000 days! That's a lot of days to try to keep the same focus in the middle of a few other competing priorities, like trying to sleep, a job, a house to keep clean, church activities, or what about just something fun and relaxing once in a while?! So, you can read this and get motivated and set out a plan, sit your little champ down and say, "This is a new day. From now on, I am going to say what I mean and mean what I say, and here are the consequences if you do not obey . . ." And you lay that out clearly. Then lunchtime comes and you lose focus and go back into old patterns, making threats and not meaning what you say, letting them run you around while you are not thinking about it, and on and on. Well, that's one day—you still have 1,999 left in this first season. There is good news in this, and it's found of all places, in Lamentations . . . doesn't sound like the place you'd go to get cheered up, but here it is:

> The steadfast love of the Lord never ceases; his mercies never come to an end; they are new every morning; great is your faithfulness. Lamentations 3:22-23 ESV

Every day is a new day with new mercies and compassion from the Lord. Yesterday is gone. Last year is gone. So, it doesn't really pay to spend much time focusing on what has been. The best thing you can do in this "Seasons" thing is jump in with each child in the season they are in and make today the best it can be! *This* is the day the Lord has made!

DIFFERENT PERSONALITIES

One of the more helpful things is to identify how *you* are made. If you are a couple raising kids, more often than not, one of you is more naturally a disciplinarian and the other is more naturally lenient . . . you get the mercies new every morning part really well and always want to go easy. In a seminar where we were teaching this, we would ask couples to identify which one was more naturally the disciplinarian and which one was more lenient, and it was usually pretty simple. This works to your great advantage because each of you will have your special season to shine. In these young years, whichever one of you is the natural disciplinarian, this is your time to step up. Work together, and more than likely, the disciplinarian will notice things getting out of hand much more quickly; pay attention.

TIME TO REGROUP

So, in our marriage, I (Rick) was more naturally the disciplinarian, and my sweet wife was just about 120% love and mercy. Now, it's not that I didn't love my kids, I did, but I just more naturally noticed if they were getting sassy or not listening. Deb understood and completely agreed with the need for them to obey with the right attitude when they were young, but her highly merciful nature could much more easily not notice when she was being led around on a leash by the ones that were probably more like me. Remember, we had 12 of them! Wait, five, but on some days . . .

Also, she was just with them more, and the daily grind of them pushing boundaries, constantly trying to get this, or whatever, could easily just desensitize her to where she just wouldn't notice. That was where my more natural bent towards discipline helped. I would see the kids sassing or running her around and I would have to point out, "Did you hear what they said?" And because she was in it more, it just became the constant drone that she forgot to pay attention to. Then I would bring it to her attention, and we would talk about it, and regroup, and make a plan and continue to implement the plan. Remember the "Mercies new every morning" part? It's true. Parenting is a marathon—and each season is actually a marathon in itself! None of us gets it right all the time. Ever. And there is so much grace built in, it's amazing.

Very often, when the kids were little, I would bring this up and we would regroup. But then, fast forward to the Fall Harvest Season when the kids were teenagers. Now, the key focuses are *Encouragement* and *Releasing*. So, guess whose personality was needed most for that season. In case you guessed Deb's, you were right. Now, I had to go against my natural bent and let go—this was *not* the season for control and discipline; this was when her merciful naturally encouraging nature was needed most. And I had to be locked in the bedroom many times. No, but I did have to be taken aside and told to calm down and relax. Which, by the way, I still didn't get a lot of that season right—stuff I figured out after the fact. I would go back and change some of these things. Deb had a more loving, encouraging, open way to handle some of our teenagers and issues that came up. But again—that speaks to the grace part, which is so encouraging!

IT'S NOT MY SEASON

So, if you are married, identify how you are wired, and recognize where you need to push into a specific season, and which season you need to listen more to your spouse. We were doing a seminar on these parenting seasons, and I identified these different personality styles and how each has their season to shine. One young couple was there and listening and they were the opposite of us; the wife was naturally the disciplinarian, and the husband was one of the most easy-going guys you could ever imagine. Sometime later we were with them, and they were having typical struggles with their little 3-year-old, and Mom was working hard to get little Junior to listen, and her husband said, "It's not my season!" We looked at each other and asked what he meant, and he said something like, "This is her season, my season's coming when they are teenagers. That's what you taught us in the seminar."

Oh, the joys of trying to communicate clearly! We were like— Whoa! You completely missed the point! It's not like you can just check out and wait for your season. Anyhow, we had a good laugh and explained it's always both of your seasons to engage—just recognize who might be more naturally wired to excel in that particular season, that person really needs to ensure discipline and obedience are happening and the other one needs to listen and pitch in.

Then, believe me, they will switch. And in the situation with this couple, when Junior is 16 and mom is ready to ground him for like 30 years, then she'll need to listen to Dad's easy-going nature and relax and increasingly release. If you recognize this, it can really help you a lot. If married, both partners need to help and be engaged during every season. If only one parent disciplines and the other seems uninvolved, one parent can feel like the "mean" parent and begin to resent the "fun" parent.

ENGAGE BOB!

It reminds me of one of my favorite movies. It's one I find a lot of inspiration and encouragement from: "The Incredibles." I'm deep like that. I'm talking about the first one that came out . . . well, now that I think about it, when all of our kids were young. Ahhh, that makes me feel better. In the movie, Mom (AKA Helen, Elastagirl, Mrs. Incredible) was the disciplinarian and Dad (AKA Bob, Mr. Incredible) was always up for a prank and an adventure. One night at dinner, the kids were out of control; Dash is picking on Violet about a boyfriend, and it erupts into a chaotic fight. Dash starts running around the table, the baby starts to fuss, and Dad is out in the other room. I guess you can be glad your kids don't have superpowers. Then, things started to escalate, and mom yelled, "Honey?!" And he gives a mumbled distracted "Kids, listen to your mother" from the other room. Then my favorite line as things are raging out of control, Mom says, "Bob, it's time to ENGAGE!"

Go ahead, look it up on YouTube "It's time to engage." Only around 10 million views; that makes me feel better too! I think the reason that's so funny is that all of us can relate. The continual challenge we have in parenting is working together—if in a home with two parents, both engaging, trying to understand each other's strength in each season.

If you are a single parent, you probably still recognize one or the other bent for yourself; this is where a close church family or small group can be a great help. Enlist the help of friends, kids' ministry leaders, youth leaders, family members—the saying, "It takes a village to raise a child" has some merit and is one reason community is so important.

DAILY ENCOURAGEMENT

Another thing you will find helpful is continually going back to some key resources. A helpful little book on biblical discipline is *Spanking: a Loving Discipline* by Roy Lessin. He gives good practical insight into how and when to use spanking, as well as when not to. Continually going back and reading little reminder "doses" of various books helped so much in staying focused.

When I (Deb) realized things were out of control and my emotions were turning often to frustration, I would realize we needed to regroup. I would literally sit down with a piece of paper and write each child's name down and beside each name, write the most frustrating thing about that kid at that moment. Sometimes there were several things.

I would pray and think and figure out a new plan; what attitude or behavior needed changing and what our plan of attack was going to be. Some days it felt as if I was in a war and had to come up with a battle plan, with five wars to be fought and won! I desperately wanted to win for my children's sake as well as mine. When the children were obedient and happy, life was pleasant. But when they were unruly and out of control, life was a drudgery and we had miserable days. I tend to like to be happy, so I did what it took to have a happy household. The saying is true, "When momma ain't happy, ain't nobody happy." We hope this book will help you and your children to have a more joy-filled life.

When the children were little, every day was so full and busy. I did not have much time for reading, so I would literally read 1-2 pages in a parenting book in the mornings before the kids got up. I usually needed a pep talk or a reminder of what I should be working on with the children. When you are constantly with the kids all day, you can tend to get immune to their whining, fighting or talking back. Reading a page or two in a parenting book kept my mind focused on what I was looking for and what I should be training them about. It was extremely helpful!

Remember, the hardest person to train in this whole scenario is us—the parent. Don't miss that. You have your habits. You have your bent. But, if you will take this to heart, and apply these tips over and over again, you will be encouraged with how these seasons unfold.

QUESTIONS FOR DISCUSSION

1. How should we work together if we are married? Discuss the two different "bents" in parents and identify how they apply in your marriage.

2. If you are a single parent, what is your natural "bent" and what are some practical and specific ways you may help to supplement that from community, friends, or family?

3. Who is the hardest person to train in parenting? What are the reasons we don't focus on this and how specifically can we prioritize and change?

4. Do you ever feel like you need to regroup? Try writing down each of your children's names and beside their name, pick the most urgent thing you want to start working with them about. Then make a plan of what to do or change and what type of discipline to do when they disobey. Having a plan is the first part of winning the battle—then carrying it out is the second.

5. Why would having a good book on these focuses to consistently read a few pages every day help you? What are other tips to keep you focused?

6. Discuss the comment about so many parents thinking their child is the "exception." What are the reasons we do that? Are there valid exceptions—what are they? Does that really mean that consistent discipline won't work? Why or why not?

CHAPTER 4

HEART

Heart is the second side of this Spring-focused coin. Like a coin always has two sides, each season has two key focuses, and they go together. While just focusing on obedience could gain the desired outward results, it is crucial that during this early Spring Season, focusing on the heart and nurturing the child's emotion and motivation is important. The goal is to get the child to *want* to obey and learn how to submit their heart and will so when they are older, they've learned how to live this way and will more readily submit to and obey God.

Part of what needs to be learned during this season is that we all live under authority. As adults, God, bosses, and government are all aspects of our authority. As children, parents primarily are. All of us struggle with this; it is the original sin. The solution is the Gospel. During this early Spring Season, we begin seeking to share the love of Jesus and who He is and what He has done to begin to see heart change. Because Jesus loved us first, we seek to honor him in our life and attitude. Think about this: Focusing only on heart without obedience produces license. Focusing only on obedience without heart brings legalism and discouragement; focusing on both heart and obedience brings liberty or freedom and sets a child off with a great start heading into the Summer Cultivation Season.

As mentioned, the heart of the "Heart" focus is the Gospel. It is during this first Spring Season that as parents, you begin modeling and explaining to your child the Gospel as soon as they can understand. The whole purpose for "obedience" is that God has a standard called God's law. But the challenge with all of us is this thing called sin. And, in all little children, because we are all born sons and daughters of Adam, is that self-centered focus. "I" is at the center of sin. Ironically, "I" is also the center of kid. As parents it is our responsibility to help our kids identify and deal with this. If we don't deal with the "I" in sin, it just continues to grow up and result in a rebellious life against God's will and His Kingdom.

THE LAW

Now, as we know, the law is in place to show all of us the standard and that we cannot ever make the mark. In fact, when Jesus taught this in the Sermon on the Mount, he even tightened it more, showing the heart of the matter behind the law: behind murder is anger (Mt. 5:21-22), behind adultery is lust (Mt. 5:27-28), behind swearing oaths, is a propensity for lying (Mt. 5:33-37), and no one is ever justified by "obedience" to God's law, the law merely points out sin (Rom. 3:20).

So, what's the point in getting into a theological discussion, we're talking about little kids here, right? As parents, it is our responsibility to train our kids for obedience and have expectations and appropriate consequences. But in doing this, what we are doing as their little minds and hearts are developing is giving them a picture of God and authority, and their challenge and bent to resist that. They want to be "god" and in control. And as you train them in that, they will go through all sorts of struggles and challenges. They will be truly sorry at times, at other times, they will try to go around you and trick you, and at other times they will outright defy you.

THE GOSPEL

During this process, you are sharing with them as young as they can begin to grasp, stories in the Bible, and who Jesus is. You begin to share that the people in the Bible weren't always obedient either and would struggle and sin. That is where grace comes in—and why Jesus came, to die in our place. As they mature through that Spring Season, and continue wrestling with obedience, as well as understanding why we need Jesus and what He did for us, there will often come a time before age seven where they will begin to understand the Gospel and want to give their lives to Jesus.

That is a great opportunity to pray with them, in their own understanding, to surrender their lives and ask Jesus to come and live in them and help them. Jesus told us we need to become like children (Mt. 18:2-4), and to let the little children come to Him and do not hinder them (Mt. 19:14). The Lord certainly honors that child-like faith, and the Holy Spirit comes into their little lives and begins to help them.

Tied into their obedience is always the Gospel. As parents, we are responsible to expect obedience while at the same time continually pointing to Jesus, where we get forgiveness and help to keep going. That is the Good News of the Gospel that changes our hearts and brings hope. Our child's understanding of this is continually maturing and developing, particularly during this first Spring Season!

HEART OBEDIENCE

We can correct a child for his wrong behavior and get him to comply to what is expected but did we win his heart? That's what we really care about. Their hearts! If we can get their little heart to *want* to obey then they will obey whether you are in the room, or they are all alone or at school or with their friends. If a child *wants* to do the right thing at three years old, he will more likely *want* to do the right thing at 13 and then at 23, all very important seasons of life.

So, while they are little adorable toddlers, we need to prioritize capturing their hearts for Jesus and train their minds to fight the lies and temptations thrown at them from the world and Satan. He wants them to throw tantrums and grow up to be self-centered. It's OK to be angry, it is not OK to kick and hit when you are angry. Jesus wants their hearts. It is our privilege to begin pointing them towards Jesus so they will have a heart desire to follow Him and do what He wants.

PRACTICAL HEART IDEAS

Most children love looking at books and having someone read to them. This is a fabulous way to train their hearts. Get your hands on any book that teaches a godly character trait. Stories or movies that show honesty, caring, praying, sharing, etc. are great as well. With all of the videos and screen time available today, *make sure they are watching intentional character-building stuff!* Some great examples are *Super-Book*, *Story-Keepers*, and *Greatest Adventures*. *Stories of the Bible* and *Listener Kids* are also excellent on YouTube. All of these pump the Truth of God's Word into their hearts and minds in ways they love to watch! Think about this—the Bible is the Truth that sets us free (John 8:31-32; 17:17) and alive and active (Heb 4:12), so intentionally putting God's Word into your little children strategically through video and audio is a powerful heart shaping strategy. And this is the time in their lives when you have the most control of making that happen. On the other hand, when you inadvertently allow your children's minds to be pumped full of hundreds of hours of disrespect, disobedience, rebellion, and the "normal" stuff that videos, games, television and movies pump into people today—naturally, this shapes their heart and who they are. That's why they call it programming.

Do. Not. Miss. This.

When our kids were young, we used *Uncle Arthur's Bed-time stories* and *Adventures in Odyssey* (in cassette tapes). Our kids loved them so much that one of our adult kids wanted us to keep the old cassette tapes and a tape recorder to play them. So, we have an old tape-recorder and those cassettes stashed away for the time when they want it for their kids—although of course now they are all digital!

Kids just love seeing and listening to kids their own age and want to follow their example. All of these are an excellent way to train children's hearts to *want* to do what they saw and heard in the videos and stories. The Bible says, "Do not be deceived: Bad company corrupts good character." (1 Cor. 15:33) One of the ways we get deceived by this is by not noticing the media they consume; that is some of the earliest "company" our kids keep and yet, so often that is treated in a lackadaisical manner. Intentionally pump "Good company" into your children's hearts and minds and it will shape their character by the Word.

GOT CHURCH?

While our kids are babies, you can get away with some hypocrisy and the kids might not be able to tell yet—but that doesn't last very long. I'd say by 3-months old you're busted. Not really—but certainly by 3 years! That is probably why so many parents that have gotten away from church, start to think about it when they have kids. There is just something about the weight of wanting to get that foundation in them that pulls on parent's hearts.

We would *highly* recommend that you make church participation a high and strong value. Particularly, in elementary children's minds, they are very literal, so they equate your worshiping in church on Sunday, and their being in a Sunday School as worshiping God. If you just go when the feeling hits you, and then you go to the beach when the feeling hits you, or you stay in bed when the feeling hits you, it creates confusion in their hearts and minds. *Give that gift of consistent prioritized church involvement to your kids!!* It creates stability and allows other adults and authority figures to speak and reinforce the same values into their little hearts.

I am personally very thankful that not one time would I ever have even imagined my parents getting up on Sunday morning and deciding to skip church because they weren't feeling it, or some other project took priority. I was literally more likely to get struck by lightning. It was just life, and a pretty good one at that. So, for my family, even on vacation, we made sure we never missed the opportunity to worship on Sundays with a congregation of God's people in church. Was it because we were so bound up or insecure that if we happened to miss church, we were going to be sucked away by the devil? Not exactly. We love worshiping with God's people and it is always refreshing to experience the body of Christ in different congregations—OK, occasionally it was downright strange, but good to expand our horizons.

The other big reason was we just wanted to make sure the kids recognized just how important it was to hear God's Word and worship God with His people every week. So, wherever we'd be traveling or on vacation, on Saturday night, we would look up churches in the area and decide which one we would go and worship with the next morning. We had some wonderful experiences—and a few interesting ones. It was so encouraging to see the body of Christ everywhere and let the kids experience that as well. We didn't want our kids to think that church is for the normal times, but when we can relax and be "off," that's the first thing to go!

I understand, this goes against the grain in our modern culture. Even people who are "committed" to a church family feel like if they are present about half the time, that is committed. It is interesting how few other areas of life that would work in; job and school come to mind first. I wonder what would happen if on Mondays people went to work when they felt like it—roughly half the time. They tell their boss that they feel this is committed to work. Their boss would have a word for that: fired! Isn't it ironic then how so many people think about half time, "when-you-feel-like-it" participation in Sunday worship is following God's instruction to be committed to the church family? They may be the only ones who believe that—it's doubtful their kids will. So, that is something to think about as you are seeking to train their hearts. Hypocrisy is one of the biggest factors that affect their heart.

Other great investments are Vacation Bible Schools as soon as they can attend, AWANA, and any other church opportunities. We'll introduce the huge value of mission trips in the upcoming seasons, but these are all critical ground preparation as you get your little seedlings started off in the best possible way!

ALL ABOUT AUTHORITY

Remember when we began this section, we said the whole human problem came by Satan challenging God's authority "Has God really said?" And, to this day, many problems in life are authority problems. While this section is about getting your little children to obey with the right hearts, I want to step back and look at some other areas of authority that ultimately really affect your kids. Since we just talked about church, we'll start there. When parents make the determination that they can be Christians but don't have to be part of a church, that is an inconsistency. It's like the finger saying, "I don't need to be connected to the body, I'm just connected to the head." Picture that. Being part of a congregation is God's design and comes with being under the protection and authority of that leadership.

As we desire our kids to respect and obey us, while we won't respect and obey local elders and deacons, that quickly becomes an inconsistency (Timothy and Titus have a lot to say about this in the Bible). Now, having been in churches for over 50 years, I have recognized one of the biggest challenges with churches is that they involve people, and all of us—dads, moms, aunts, cousins, preachers, elders, deacons—are messed up to some degree. And so there has to be patience and forgiveness. That's not to say there is never a time to move on, but if the kids grow up hearing you bash the preacher on the drive home, or complain about the elders, (we'll get to dad's and mom's next) what message are they getting? We go to church and put on a good "face" but behind the back of authority, we are cynical and critical. The kids realize that Mom and Dad's hearts aren't with them. That has a very negative effect on the children's hearts.

AUTHENTICITY

One of the things I really appreciate about my own parents is that I can never remember a snide or critical remark about our church's leadership growing up. They simply had sincere hearts in wanting to live in and under the God-given authority of their church. I didn't think anything about it, but they just humbly wanted to be supportive, and I know it's not because everybody was perfect, and everything was always done right. There was a sincerity and authenticity there that was genuine. That probably had at least something to do with why all four of my sisters and I grew up following the Lord.

There is something particularly damaging to a child's heart when they see two-faced hypocrisy. Acting all sappy and spiritual in one setting but then on a dime, switching and mocking and complaining about the same people you were just smiling with really messes with a child. And this is not about perfection or super spirituality, it's just about consistency and authenticity. We've known different families through the years where the dad was rude, harsh and crabby. But interestingly, these dads weren't all sweet faced around us or smiley at church—they were just always rude, harsh and crabby. They were pretty much an equal opportunity offender; what you saw was what you got, pretty much every time.

Here is the fascinating part, all of their children have grown up following the Lord and are ironically, relatively happy! What's up with that? There was consistency. Sure, Dad had challenges, we all have challenges, but he wasn't a hypocrite. They genuinely took their faith seriously and they were working it out in an authentic, predictable, consistently crabby way.

HONOR YOUR PARENTS

We once heard Bruce Wilkinson say something to the effect of, "If you don't want your kids to rebel against you, then they better never hear you speak negatively about your parents. If that's your attitude toward your parents, why would you expect them to have a good attitude towards you!?" That struck us to the heart. Up to that time, we would just say negative things or complain about our parents whenever something came to mind, but from that point on, we determined never to say a negative word about either of our parents around our kids. Now in bed we would complain all night long . . . just kidding. But if we wanted to discuss those things, we would do it in private.

That was a very great insight to us. Why *would* we think we could sow disrespect towards our own parents and somehow reap respect from our kids? We had just never thought about it before. When the Bible says, "You reap what you sow" that is using a farming metaphor to speak of consequences. You're free to live any way you want, but you are not free to avoid the consequences of your choices. Sow disrespect to your parents now and plan to reap respect from your kids later? That's about as likely as planting potatoes and hoping to harvest green beans.

All of these seasons build on the prior, and we can choose any way we want to do them. The challenge with seasons of parenting, is that the consequences often don't show up until about eight years later, after two seasons have passed. So, it pays to think carefully about it now and choose wisely.

YOUR EXAMPLE

We should be aware that our kids model our attitudes and actions. How you respond to the driver that cuts in front of you, will be noticed by your small children. One Mom was driving and heard her little girl from the back car-seat ask, "Mommy, where are all the idiots?" and Mom said, "Oh honey, they only come out when Daddy drives." Ouch. How you talk to and about the grouchy drive thru employee will be how your children treat their friends. How you talk about your boss will affect how they respect their boss, which at the moment ironically is you! How you react and treat your spouse will be how they treat their siblings, and likely their spouse one day. Some good questions to ask yourself are would you like your son to be treated like you treat your husband? Would you like your daughter to be treated like you treat your wife?

A few nights ago, I was carrying my water glass and plate of spaghetti to the table and the plate slipped out of my hand and dropped spilling spaghetti all over me, the table and the floor. I like a lot of sauce! Trying to save that then caused the drink glass to slip out of my other hand, shattering glass and water all over the spaghetti sauce. It was just beautiful. I got aggravated and started raising my voice and Deb said, "Grandpa, you've got five sets of eyes really watching you right now." It's amazing how often the Holy Spirit sounds just like my wife! We had five of the grandkids and they were all sitting down right there beside us, eating their curds and whey.

Then yesterday, Shelby was over spending some time with Deb and she told the *whole story* she learned from her kids. Tessa was telling them in great detail what happened and she said, "And then Grandpa lost his emotions!" No. Kidding. Very shortly after this, some friends from church stopped by to borrow some chairs and I went out to help them and they were alarmed and thought I was bleeding because not realizing it, I still had spaghetti sauce all over my ankle—it just doesn't stop.

Training their hearts has so much to do with attitude and much of it is caught from who you really are. They are *always* watching; and just when you think you're done, five grandkids are staring at you losing your emotions! We as parents (and grandparents) need to check our hearts and attitudes and daily actions. Are you displaying the fruit of the Spirit? Our kids are totally going to model their actions, and perhaps more importantly, attitudes, after us. If you don't like their tone of voice that they talk to their siblings with, check how you talk to them or to their daddy. Do they have trouble getting along with others at school or church? Do they explain situations as though they are always the wronged victim? Think back over how you talk about your neighbors or friends. They are learning from someone and in the earliest years, it is mostly you. So, this is a big area for us as parents to work on ourselves for the sake of how we want our children to grow up to be. It can be difficult to hear and even more challenging to apply.

HEART TRAINING ACTIVITIES

Some suggestions are to go to an elderly person's house and visit, taking your kids with you. Have your kids make a picture or help you make cookies to take to them. Go pull weeds for your grandparents and have them help. Teach them to share their snack with someone with a happy heart, telling them that Jesus likes it when we share. It makes Him happy when we are kind to others, and that makes us happy! He was always helping others.

Teach them they have the power to make choices to be happy or sad. When someone does something to upset them, instead of continuing to harbor angry bitter feelings, talk them through how to feel their feelings but don't stop there. Then show them how to let it go and teach them they have the choice to make in their own thoughts to forgive. That might be worth re-reading. They have to choose it.

I (Deb) just did this recently. I was driving with a little girl who had hurt feelings about being left out of taking a turn playing with a certain toy—tears and the whole thing! I decided this was a great teaching moment. I stopped the car, pulled over to a parking place and walked around to her side of the car and quietly talked to her. I said, "God gives us the power to choose happy thoughts or sad thoughts. We get to choose. What are your tears about?" She told me what was upsetting her. I caringly listened and told her I totally understand how that hurt her feelings and then suggested an alternative to the situation and she was happy with it. She smiled and I did too. But then I said, "Now you get to choose if you are going to forgive and let it go and choose to be happy, or do you want to be sad? You can decide." She said, "I want to be happy." Then we went on our way.

That is a heart-shaping moment. Rather than just looking in the back seat and saying, "Stop crying!" or something to that effect, it's better to stop, take time and share with them so they have the right attitude; we call it a "happy heart." Taking time for these moments is priceless. They are really more valuable than anything else you can do. Any time you can turn a daily life moment into a time of teaching them a heart lesson, it's totally worth the time. Daily things that happen between siblings, like fighting, and taking each other's toys can be turned into heart training. It's helpful to use Scripture to talk about why we don't want them to act a certain way.

A resource that you will want to go back to again and again to help you keep their heart in focus is *Shepherding Your Child's Heart* by Tedd Trip. While there are endless books you can read out there, we will give you just a few that we have found to be helpful in each season. And then, because this is such a marathon—and particularly in those small years during that Spring Season, it will be helpful to just continually give yourself regular—and sometimes daily—reminders to keep you focused.

MUTUAL RESPECT

Treat your child with respect and lots of love and they will more naturally want to please you. If they feel loved and cared for, their hearts will be soft toward you, making obeying you easier. It is extremely important to speak positively, give compliments, and try never to use degrading words or tones. Make sure they *feel* special. Look in their eyes when they talk to you; put down your phone and really listen. Pay attention when they are talking, bend down and take a knee so you can be eye to eye sometimes. Take them on one-on-one dates so they can have *all* your attention. Do activities that they enjoy together, buy them small treats, give gifts when they don't expect it, all these things will turn their hearts toward you. We don't mean every time you go somewhere, or they become entitled, stop appreciating it and just expect it, but mix it up—utilizing all the elements of this paragraph across their little lives.

One thing I (Rick) love about this Spring Season, is you can take them to Dollar Tree and tell them they are free to get anything they want in the whole store! They feel like they are on top of the world, and you are only out a dollar. But I have noticed that the effect does start to wear off pretty rapidly as they grow, and recently it became the 1.25 store. Inflating prices, deflating results—this is definitely a bummer!

Always seeking to treat your kids with respect has a really big impact on their heart. It is interesting though how we can naturally treat our wife or kids with much less respect than we would our co-workers or friends, and yet we love and care more about our spouse and kids than them. I suppose it is familiarity. How often I have yelled at my kids or heard other parents barking disrespectfully to their kids—and this is in public. It humiliates them around their friends or other respected adults and *withers their hearts* and their courage.

Praise them in public and correct them in private. If you want to make them feel respected, this is a good motto to keep in mind.

THE INTERRUPT RULE

Another way to treat them with respect is to teach them the "Interrupt rule." Most children have trouble waiting to talk when they have something on their mind to say, or simply when they want attention. It makes them feel honored when you teach them how to wait their turn to talk and then you actually give them priority to talk and you listen intently to what they are saying.

Here's how it works. Teach the child to put their hand on your forearm or leg while you are talking or someone else is talking to you. Then you immediately place your hand on top of their hand, so they know without a doubt that you know they are there and that they want to talk. It's your *secret code* that you share together. As soon as there is a pause in the adult conversation, seize the opportunity to look at your child and compliment them for waiting and being so patient, and then say, "What did you want to say?" Then listen to them attentively. The child feels valued and honored and they are not constantly interrupting your conversations.

I actually just did this with a child this past weekend and I could see in her reaction how it made her feel. She almost grew in height when I complimented her on how proud I was of how she waited patiently. She continued using our new *secret code* throughout the weekend. I think it really made her happy. All these things encourage a child's heart while maintaining discipline and order.

GUAGING THE HEART

Constantly paying attention to the attitude of your children is gauging their heart behind their actions. Once you train obedience into them, it should seem normal to live in that environment of authority with peace and contentment. An example of gauging the heart would be something like this:

Little Suzie is having fun playing with her friends and Mom says, "It's time to go home." Now Suzie's playing has been interrupted. Here are two different ways this can go:

1) Immediately Suzie goes from happily playing to crying. Now Mom gets frustrated and asks, "Why are you crying?" She says "Because you said we have to go home!!! Waaaaaaah!!!!!!!!!!!" As she lets rip extra loud bursts of crying and sad faces.

2) Suzie is sad that they have to stop playing and go home but she has been taught to reign in her self-will and her actions to what her authority (mom) has taught her. She has practiced at home and is learning how to deny her own urges to get what she wants. She has an inner struggle but can bring herself to say, "OK Mommy."

These types of scenarios play out continually with three variations.

1) Children are not taught or expected to obey—much of the time the parents obey their children, and when they are challenged, well prepare for World War III!

2) Children are taught to obey and generally do, but with an inner protest. They might reluctantly be getting ready to go but their

face is scowling, their feet are dragging or stomping . . . all indicators of "obedience" but not a right "heart" behind it.

3) Children are taught to obey, with consistency and careful attention given to attitude, folding in the Gospel. The child naturally has a struggle giving up their will but in general, they are happy to obey and recognize this is just normal.

Of course, our goal is to make that third outcome normal as we continually gauge their hearts, praying for and encouraging the right attitude behind the actions. We can train for all of these types of moments at home. Then when we are out of the home with friends and family, or shopping, the whole family has a pleasant experience because all these moments have been worked on in advance at home. That is intentional rather than reactive parenting. Now they know how to respond in a way that makes themselves genuinely happy and therefore it makes Mom happy too. We are always working on teaching them that obeying Mommy is training them for obeying the Lord when He tells them to do something. We want to be continually paying attention to their hearts. Once that becomes normal and expected, they are much better trained and ready for the next Summer Season of super growth!

QUESTIONS FOR DISCUSSION

1. "Bad company corrupts good character." Is the company your children keep through their screen time something that is building a godly or worldly heart? What are specific things you should cut out for them? What specific sources should you add in? How and when will you implement this?

2. How do children feel when we as parents decide to skip church? In what ways would this affect their view of God?

3. What are the ways you are being a spiritual example to your children? Do they see you living out your faith—reading the Bible, praying, giving, serving and helping others, etc.?

4. Which of your attitudes and actions do you want your children to imitate? When do you most often "lose your emotions?"

5. Would you want your kids to grow up with the same attitude towards you that you currently display about your parents? Specifically, how should or shouldn't you change this?

6. Have you thought about showing your children respect? How can you do this while still being the authority in their lives?

7. Which of the outcomes and variations on the last two pages is most like your kids when you say, "It's time to go home?" If it's not the last on both lists, discuss what you can do to change that.

CHAPTER 5

ALWAYS IN SEASON

Certain things are always in season—like praying for your kids, having fun, being actively involved in a local church, and providing love as the foundation for the home. On the other hand, there are qualities that parents may think are always in season, but they are not. These are the right thing, but the wrong time—such as using your authority in discipline, giving choices, spending too much time on reasoning, trying to be your little child's "friend." These are all great things, but only when done in the right season.

There are certain things in farming that are always in season. Sunshine is always in season, spring, summer, fall and winter. Sure, you have cloudy days, but the sun is always needed. Fresh air— always in season. Good soil—that's always in season. Rain, it's always needed; granted, in some more than others, but always in season. We want to point out certain activities in parenting that are to be present from birth, really until you die.

LOVE

Of course, it almost goes without saying, but love is certainly always in season. I think of 1 Corinthians 13, where it says if you give everything you have away, if you have faith that moves mountains, have the best knowledge, if you even give your body to be burned in self-sacrifice, and you don't have love you are . . . nothing! Not less than, not diminished, but nothing! That is strong.

So, love is more important than any of these other activities in this book. 1 Corinthians chapter 13 shows us what this love looks like:

Love is patient
Love is kind
Love is not jealous
Love is not boastful or proud
Love is not rude
Love doesn't demand its own way
Love is not irritable
Love keeps no record of being wronged
Love doesn't rejoice about injustice, but rejoices whenever the truth wins out
Love never gives up
Love never loses faith
Love is always hopeful
Love endures through every circumstance (NLT)

Now that's a lot of love! The Bible says love covers a multitude of sins, so with plenty of love, a lot of other things work out. But here is something that really encourages me. In all of these qualities in this list, God is first that way with me, and you. The Bible says God loved us first—while we were in rebellion; we didn't love him, he loved us (Rom 5:8, 1 Jn 4:10) and this is how God's love looks towards us; He is patient, He is kind, He never gives up, He is always hopeful. Even when we are not, He is! What a great foundation for us to build love into all seasons of our parenting, knowing how God treats and views us! The more we apply everything in this book in this way of love— patiently, kindly, not boasting, etc.—the better it all goes! And God has given us His Spirit to work out that love as a fruit in our own lives. (Gal 5:22)

In his book *How Children Raise Parents*, Dan Allender says kids are always asking basically two questions of parents: "Do you love me?" and "Can I have my own way?" And with that, there are four possible combinations, ranked in order from best to worst. The best one is: Do you love me? YES. Can I have my own way? NO. That is what we are espousing in this book. Love with consistent boundaries and discipline produces the most secure child and peaceful environment for that child to thrive in. If, particularly in this Spring Season from birth through six, you make your main focus that the answer to the first question, "Do you love me?" is a resounding yes in your child's heart and mind, and the answer to the second question, "Can I have my own way?" is an equally resounding no for them, then those little sprouts are in the best possible place to receive the *Vision & Teaching* of summer and then *Releasing* and *Encouraging* in fall. In their little hearts, they desire both of those answers to have the most peace in their lives, even though they do not understand it in their minds.

The second-best combination was this: Do you love me? YES. Can I have my own way? YES. That would be a loving but permissive environment. Because love is *so* important, it better covers over the absence of discipline, although discipline is love (Heb. 12:4-11). This would be the environment I (Rick) was raised in. I knew I was very loved but had very little discipline. I got more spankings from my sisters, who were old enough to be my mom, than I ever did from my parents because I was a spoiled brat. One time I remember mouthing Dad and he gave me a kick in the butt, which I totally deserved. It seems to have worked out OK, but I have probably struggled more with discipline in my life as a result of that environment. So, I just blame that on my parents—you know you have to be the victim of something these days.

The third best combination of the four was: Do you love me? NO. Can I have my own way? NO. This would be a harsh and unloving environment but with strict boundaries and discipline. Strict boundaries without the all-important quality of love are very damaging. However, it is still better than the last combination, because discipline in and of itself shows some care and love.

The worst possible combination is: Do you love me? NO. Can I have my own way? YES. This was characteristic of the completely unengaged parent—they paid little attention, showed no love and the kids run the streets with no boundaries at all, basically raising themselves. There isn't even enough care to pay attention to any boundaries. I thought that was helpful to show how important love is when combining and ranking both love and discipline.

You've probably heard about *The Five Love Languages* by Gary Chapman. They also have *The Five Love Languages of Children*. I (Deb) had each of our kids take the five Love Languages test and found it to be extremely helpful as a busy mom of five. Once I found out each child's love language, I could just do the top activity that felt like love for each child. It made me feel super-efficient! I started to try to focus my efforts on showing each child daily love in their own love language and I had more peace in knowing they were feeling loved in the best way.

PRAY

A major priority to include throughout every season is praying for your children. Make it your goal to pray every day for each of your children. Seriously, this is more important than any other thing in this book, with the exception of love. It is you as the parent, lifting up your child to God in faith, and God working 24-7 on them in ways you cannot comprehend.

Job was a guy in the Bible from the land of Oz—wait, that was a different story—the land of Uz. When Satan, that old accuser came to God to accuse Job, God said that there was no one on earth like Job who was blameless and upright (Job 1:8). Then apart from stating how much wealth and influence he had, the only example of his righteous acts was his interceding on behalf of his children. You would think a lot of different examples could have been included from the guy God said "there was no one on earth" like him—but that is how important this is!

Pray for their hearts. Pray for protection from the evil one. Pray for wisdom from God to help you to know what to do and how to do it. That's a big one! Half of the battle is us as parents having the ability to see what to do and do it. Ask God to open your eyes to this; that's wisdom! Every day—pray, pray, pray! The Bible is very clear that there is an unseen world and war going on and God along with his legions of angels are at work as well as demonic hosts (Eph. 6). Amazingly, the Bible says one of the angel's big jobs is to serve us, delivering and protecting! (Heb. 1:14, 2 Kings 6:17-20) We often forget the spiritual realities going on around us.

I remember when our oldest daughter Leah was probably eight, Deb had dropped me off at guitar lessons and then she and the kids jumped in the minivan for a short errand. She was driving down Clinton Street, the main one-way 4-lane thoroughfare in Ft Wayne Indiana. Leah was sitting on the front passenger seat when suddenly the passenger door came open and she fell out at probably 35-40mph! Deb just saw her little ponytail flying around in the rear-view mirror as she rolled down the highway with four lanes of oncoming headlights at dusk. Amazingly, all of the traffic just stopped in a line across all four lanes. Of course, Deb stopped as soon as she could and ran back to check on Leah who was just sitting in the middle of the road. Deb asked Leah if she was OK, and she said yes and then she said, "The man stopped the traffic." And Deb said, "What man?" By this time there was a semi driver who had stopped and walked up, and Deb said, "This guy?" And Leah said, "No, an old man with long gray hair was standing right in the middle of the road with both hands up in the air stopping the traffic!" They all looked around, and no one saw anyone like that—but he was there, at just the right time, and then he was gone. I just talked with Leah yesterday about this and it's still a vivid memory.

Another time, quite a few years later, our oldest son Justin was playing hide and seek with one of his friends who had come over. He was probably 14 at the time, and got a not-so-bright idea to throw our big metal dog cage into the swimming pool, and get in it to hide, perhaps thinking the weight of the cage would keep him down? When he got in, the door of the cage was on the top, but the current of the water and motion caused the cage to turn over to where the door was now on the bottom and there was nothing Justin could do to get out. He threw himself back and forth in the cage, trying to get it to turn over and he was thrashing around on the bottom of the pool. Nothing was working and he was quickly running out of breath. He remembers thinking this was how he was going to die!

In the meantime, his friend who was doing the "finding" was upstairs in our bathroom in the middle of "Number 2." At that moment he had an unmistakable urging that said, "Go look in the swimming pool!" He jumped up right in the middle of the job and ran downstairs and looked in the pool, only to see a cage on the bottom with Justin in it! He dove in and grabbed the cage, bringing Justin to the surface saving his life! Just another minute or two and the story would have been much different. While there is certainly plenty of mystery in all of this, there is an unseen world that God is at work in, and He calls us to pray into this, interceding for our kids!

Jesus said in the model "Lord's prayer" that we are to pray for deliverance and protection from the enemy—because God intervenes supernaturally in our lives somehow in response to our prayers (Mt. 6:13). I think so many of us overlook this—but Jesus put it right in his model prayer, and when He was praying for His disciples before His crucifixion, he prayed twice that they would be protected from the evil one. (John 17:11,15)

James says our prayers are powerful and effective (Jas 5:16). Sometimes God answers our prayers the way we would like, and sometimes He doesn't—but He certainly isn't responding to our prayers, if we do not believe or prioritize enough to pray. Also, and amazingly, it also seems they are stored up even from one generation to the next. Revelation speaks of the elders at the end of time "holding golden bowls full of incense, which are the prayers of God's people" seemingly still having impact! (Rev 5:8)

One thing I really appreciated about my (Rick's) own mother is that she really prayed for us. From as little as I could remember when it was bedtime, she would be on her knees beside her bed praying . . . and praying . . . and praying. It felt like forever! She would pray every night for all of her children, and then grandchildren, and eventually great grandchildren and finally great great grandchildren. I really attribute a lot of the remarkable blessing and protection our family has experienced to her faithful prayers.

In 1944 it was just my Dad and Mom having their first little baby Patty. Now just a little over 75 years later, their immediate family is 230 of us, nearly all following Christ! You'd think we were rabbits—or at least Catholics. But nope, just passionate Protestants! (as my brother-in-law Steve liked to say when asked if they were Catholics with their 10 kids) Don't ever underestimate the impact of your prayers on parenting in the mundane day-to-day—it will compound greatly over time. Far more important than these seasonal principles is the power of prayer and God acting in your children's lives!

A wonderful book to learn how to pray for your kids is *The Power of Praying for Your Children* by Stormie Omartian—don't let her name scare you; as far as we can tell, she's not stormy or a Martian. Deb has used that book to pray for our kids for years. And still does with *The Power of Praying for Your Adult Children* and *The Power of Praying for Your Grandchildren.*

CHERISH YOUR SPOUSE

If you are married, this is a major and often overlooked quality. So often, parents will focus on their children while neglecting their marriage. It is easy to do this because of all the demands and it can even feel right because we love our kids so much and want the best for them. Don't miss this: *One of the very best things you can do in parenting your children is to cherish your spouse.* When your kids see you Dad, loving your wife, putting her first, taking her out on dates while they get left behind with a sitter—all of these things build into your children an inner peace and confidence. Now of course they may fuss and whine when you don't put them first but don't ever be shy to express through your example and sometimes your words that their mother is your first priority. God says "Husbands, love your wives as Christ loved the church and gave himself up for her." He didn't say, "Husbands, love your children first and devote everything to them." And guess what, before you sleep about twice, the kids will be gone, and their mother will still be there, at least that's how it's supposed to be. How often have we heard of marriages falling apart after the children leave because they didn't invest in each other, or they even stayed together just for the kids. An honest and aware child really wants nothing more than for Dad and Mom to truly love one another; that brings a strong foundation and real security to their world.

Apart from one really rough year, I may have enough fingers to count the weeks thru our 36 years of our marriage where Deb and I have not gone out on a date. It's funny how we will date before we are married and then somehow think it doesn't matter anymore. It actually matters more. Now you're married and you need to make it work, keeping the love alive! When the kids were young, I'd always make sure Deb arranged a sitter so we could go out every week. There were many reasons why not to do this: we couldn't afford it, there were so many other things going on, the kids didn't want us to and on and on. Different times Deb would say, "Honey, we can't afford a sitter!" I remember telling her we can't afford not to, this is a lot cheaper than marriage counseling, which we had learned from experience (that was the really rough year). We became the masters at the cheap date, sharing meals and finding deals. Now that the kids are gone, we get to go out several times a week and it's one of the most enjoyable things we do.

In the same way, Mom, when your kids see you respecting and honoring your husband, you can know that you are doing one of the best things possible for your children. We are trying to teach our kids to obey and respect authority, and what is more powerful than modeling that in a tangible way first in your marriage? If the kids see you treating Daddy with respect and honor, they most likely will too. The kids should not even think for a second that they can get Dad and Mom to go against each other, pitting one against the other. Don't ever go to your kids and secretly complain about your spouse, they need to see you as a united force.

For example, every family has children that ask Mom for a candy and Mom says "No, it's almost time for dinner." Then the child goes to Dad and asks Dad for candy, and he says yes. Then he finds out later that Mom said no. The best way to avoid these situations is to ask the child what the other parent said before giving an answer. Always back each other in front of the kids, even if you don't agree.

Then privately talk about your differences when it comes to the children so that you can be on the same page. This will be the healthiest option for your kids—you really don't want your kids to see you arguing about them as this can cause emotional turmoil.

When you prioritize your marriage and cultivate a strong united bond between the two of you by investing there first, many things within your entire family take their proper place.

PLAY

Creating an environment where there is laughter, playfulness, and cheer is very powerful throughout a child's entire life. Proverbs 17:22 says, "A cheerful heart is good medicine, but a crushed spirit dries up the bones."

Now, obviously, we know life isn't always fun. In fact, it's often stressful. But notice the second part of Prov. 17:22, "A crushed spirit dries up the bones." Without cheer, fun, and relaxation, life can be heavy for a child—actually, for anyone. So, build in the fun. In a prior book I wrote, *Lasting Leadership*, studying the lives of pastors whose marriage and families stood the test of time, and all of their children grew up loving and following the Lord, one of the key findings was that they all built in fun. For some, it came more naturally. For others, they had to be intentional about taking days off and just playing and de-stressing with the family. One of the family's adult children remembered that they would go to the airport and just ride the tram for no other reason than to just have fun, all talking in a fake southern accent, pretending that they were from Alabama or somewhere. Corny stuff—but that made an impact. It was good medicine!

When our kids were young, we would go on camping trips. I bought the biggest tent I could find, and it was a great time to play.

We'd do special traditions each year like a leaf hunting contest, where I would set out the rules that we would judge the best red leaf, green, yellow, brown, most unique item, etc. and they would come back for the judging and winning prize, which was usually something like a bigger treat at Dairy Queen. Somehow, we always found a creek or mud-hole and the boys would be completely black with mud with just two little white eyes showing.

We started a tradition when our first, Leah was just a baby, of going to a Christmas tree farm in Ft. Wayne Indiana to cut down our own Christmas tree. It was always the Friday after Thanksgiving, and it became a yearly tradition for the next 25 years. We found different Christmas tree farms through the years, but they would often have holiday music, gift shop, festive holiday food, and activities.

Once we got to the Christmas tree farm, we would pick up the saw and measuring stick and go out hunting for the perfect tree. Sometimes they had a cute train or trailer to take us out into the farm. Then, when we would find the perfect tree, we would all line up and go around the tree three times dancing and hollering. It probably looked pretty crazy, but it was just a goofy tradition, and the kids laughed and danced. The older they got; it became a little more embarrassing, OK, a lot more embarrassing. I remember when our oldest daughter got married and we went out to the Christmas tree farm, Joey thought we were nuts and finally the whole family revolted once and for all, and we had to stop the tradition. Just corny stuff. After we'd get the tree, we'd eat lunch out as a family and come home and set it up. Holidays are a great time to create your own family traditions that your kids will love.

During the Christmas season, one night we always slept under and around the Christmas tree, baked Christmas cookies, and made a big deal about the Christmas stockings. Even today if our adult kids are sleeping overnight on Christmas morning, they know they will get a stocking—and it's interesting how they still seem to enjoy trying to make that happen.

We made a huge Thanksgiving Blessing Tree and put it up on our wall every Thanksgiving. Most mornings leading up to Thanksgiving, each child would get a construction paper leaf and they got to write what they were thankful for. By the end of the season, we had a big colorful tree highlighting all the blessings we had to be thankful for!

In the winter up in Indiana, when there was snow, we would go to Interstate 69 where there was a huge hill by the clover-leaf exit, and we would take sleds and slide down the hill over and over until we were frozen. Then we would all stop in at Heyerly's Bakery and get donuts and hot chocolate. All of these things were fun, memory building traditions that bonded us together.

Plan family fun nights. We would often go to Chuck E. Cheese and had fun playing the games and adding up the tickets to see what junk—I mean prizes—we could go home with. Movie nights at home with popcorn and staying up a little later was always a big hit. Roller skating, ice skating, ditches, trees, creeks, beaches, amusement parks, neighborhood parks, pottery classes, guitar and piano lessons, bike rides—all of these activities are fun for kids. Incorporating some of these types of fun into every week can provide a relief for your kids and family from all the pressures and stress of life.

For some reason, I enjoy mowing the yard. I think it's because it's one of the few things in my life I see instant results in! When I'm mowing—and I just have a small push mower; when I grow up, I have dreamed of getting one of those nice zero turns, but for now—I'll be walking behind, and it has the mulch feature that keeps all the grass under the deck to get the grass real fine and make the yard look nice. But then there are sometimes, when the grass is so long or wet, or the blades are dull, that it just starts to bog down and kills the mower. During those times, I have a trick that makes all the difference. I'll take something like a palm branch laying around (just had to say that for all my family in Indiana) and prop up the side shoot so that the grass is able to get out, and then I can get through about anything and keep on going.

Fun, play, and laughter are like a relief valve; like opening the side shoot—you can get bogged down, clogged up, and your blades can get pretty dull, but if you keep having fun, keep laughing and playing along the way, it lessens the pressure and provides the relief that helps you keep going! School life for your children can be very stressful and bog them down. Planning something fun in the evening after dinner will be more valuable than you can imagine. Actively playing and engaging the old-fashioned way, without phones and screens is like opening the shoot to relieve stress in your kids' lives!

CHURCH

Living your life in the context of a church family is always in season. It provides the other relationships that help you keep focused on God and to work out normal life challenges, as well as the biblical values and structure that help a family to mature. The Bible says:

> And let us consider how we may spur one another on toward love and good deeds, not giving up meeting together, as some are in the habit of doing, but encouraging one another—and all the more as you see the Day approaching.
> Hebrews 10:24-25

How do you continually spur each one in your family on toward love and good deeds—by meeting together and encouraging one another. When parents neglect that at any point in their lives—they naturally, by their example, discourage the love and good works within God's family.

Young children in particular naturally equate church and God together in their young minds. One day a little boy talked with me (Deb) and said in a very concerned way, "I'm afraid everyone in my family has forgotten about God except me." I was shocked to hear his concern at such a young age. He said, "It doesn't seem like my mom and dad want to go to church anymore. We always stay home and just play instead of going to church! I don't know what to do to get them interested in God again."

Give that child long enough without the influence of a church family, and he too will likely forget God—at least in any practical sense. I never forgot an impacting object lesson when I was a teenager and we were at a youth group bonfire outside on a summer evening. One of the pastors was there talking about the importance of staying connected to the church family. Before his talk, he took a red-hot log off of the bonfire and set it to the side. Then after his short talk, he pointed out that the log which had been red hot and on fire just a few minutes earlier was now cooled down, black and just smoking. He made an impacting point that in the absence of the other logs, it couldn't stay lit! God has designed the church congregation to keep encouraging us towards following the Lord, like the logs need each other to keep burning. If we give up meeting together, we do so to our own detriment, and even more so—the detriment of our children.

There you have some things that are always in season: Loving, praying, cherishing your spouse, playing, and living your life in a local congregation of believers.

QUESTIONS FOR DISCUSSION

1. Of the five "Always in Season" activities: Loving, praying, cherishing your spouse, playing, and living your life in a local congregation of believers, which one impacted you the most? What are the reasons?

2. Which of the "Always in Season" activities comes easiest or most naturally to you? Which one comes hardest or is the most easily left out?

3. In the "Love" section, two questions every child wants the answer to were asked: Do you love me? And can I have my own way? Of those four combinations of answers, how were you raised? What are some practical things you could do to move your own family towards answering "Yes" to love and "No" to having my own way?

4. What are some practical rhythms and habits you already do or could build into your life to help you pray for each of your children every day?

5. James 1:5 says if we lack wisdom, just ask and you'll get it. How specifically could consistently praying for wisdom in parenting make a difference?

6. How is playing together important for your family? What are some special things you do?

CHAPTER 6

CHANGING SEASONS

June 21st is the first day of summer. September 23rd is the first day of fall. While we know these shifts happen on a specific day, with slight variations, none of us wakes up the next morning and just automatically says, "Wow, it's fall today. Honey, did you know it's fall today?" No, if you are like me and someone asked you what day summer or fall starts, you would have no idea. I just asked Google. The truth is the seasons have been changing for many weeks and you can sense that. I'll say things like, "I love this weather—fall is in the air!" Well, when it comes to seasons of parenting, the same is true as well.

We just went through the Spring Season with the focus of *Obedience* and *Heart*. Now we are moving into the Summer Season and the two key focus areas in this season are *Teaching* and *Vision*.

We have given ages when these seasons end and begin, but much like the exact beginning day of summer, the truth is that it is gradual with overlapping in the case of parenting seasons as well. Here is a chart that I want to unpack for you:

CHANGING SEASONS CHART

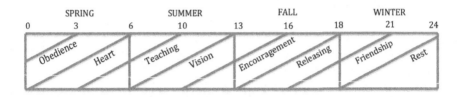

Here you see represented all four seasons with different ages written across the top. Take a few moments to study this. You'll notice rising lines with a main focus listed directly below it. In each of these seasons, the two key focuses are applied with about a 3-year difference in when they are starting and when they are peaking. Initially, this might seem confusing. Like that chart at first glance might look as if it is crooked and angling down, it is perfectly level. Likewise, getting the timing and focus correct in *Seasons of Parenting* are not always what they appear on the surface. It will take some focused concentration, but it will be worth it. Let me unpack it from left to right.

We just covered spring—birth through six years old. The two focus areas are *Obedience* and *Heart* during that season, but you'll notice they are separated. Focusing on your little guy's ability to obey you begins just as soon as he is able to start understanding, and then you apply those training sessions that Deb talked about. But that peaks already by three years old which means now you are in maximum focus and concentration. At three, your little guy can understand you, is talking and walking and probably talking back and walking or running away. This is prime time to implement discipline and focus there. At three you are fully implementing obedience training and you continue on with that. The *Heart* focus begins just a little later as their understanding and emotions mature a bit more, so you are really paying attention to their heart attitude at about three but peaking in focus and concentration around six.

Now, notice something else in the upcoming Summer Season where *Teaching* and *Vision* are the key focuses from 7-13. The *Teaching* focus involves academic teaching and biblical world-view teaching. The technical transition between spring and summer is their 7th birthday. Often "1st Grade" is at seven years old, but that isn't the first time they have been learning—there is Kindergarten, and sometimes pre-school. In the same way, you don't wait until they are seven to begin teaching them God's Word and Bible stories—no, that really begins earlier, very intentionally like around three where that line starts on the bottom of the chart. You have them watch good Bible-based cartoons, read them Bible stories and many resources we'll introduce in the next section, all of that starting about the middle of the Spring Season. You are at peak focus and concentration with that value about the middle of summer around 10. Notice that the other focus during summer, *Vision*, doesn't start that early. It begins a little later as you start sprinkling it in at the beginning of summer around seven but it peaks right around 13, just when the teen "harvest" years begin and that vision is now going to be lived out. At that point, they should have a clear vision of the path ahead. The same goes for the following values in the remaining seasons.

Notice something else. When those ascending diagonal lines peak, they don't go back down, they remain as you seek to maintain what has been built into them. Now, the further you go, the less concentration you are giving to that focus area. Let me explain. When you begin to implement discipline and expect obedience when they are very young, you and the child still expect obedience through the Summer Season elementary age, however it has been normal now for quite some time and now all you do is periodically reinforce it.

Maintaining takes less effort than initiating. During the teen years, it is still important, but your reinforcement is far less frequent or effective and if you wait to start there, it has the opposite desired effect.

Another example is *Vision*. While that begins to be introduced at the beginning of summer and peaks at the beginning of fall, you continue maintaining that vision throughout the teenage years. However, now you are actually applying the fall focuses of *Encouragement* and *Releasing* as you help them to carry out what has now become *their* vision. Each one builds upon the prior, and when the earlier focus peaks in concentration, it stays important, although your effort and intentionality will become less. That is why it is so important to get these established at the right time so later you can merely maintain them, while adding the next. Each preceding focus provides the ideal environment for the following focuses to be added in, at the right time and in the right order. As I said, it's a lot to digest.

All of this will make more sense as we go through each season and we encourage you to refer back to this later, but we wanted to introduce these transitioning seasons and when each focus begins and peaks. Now on to summertime!

QUESTIONS FOR DISCUSSION

1. Spend a few moments studying the Changing Seasons Chart. What age does "Vision" begin to get introduced? What age should it be maximized and completed?

2. How many years are there between when a focus value is started and completed? Notice how you begin to implement the focus a little bit and increase that over a six-year period. Why could it be a tendency to do too much too soon so that you peak early, instead of steadily increasing and maintaining the focus over the entire six years?

3. Once the focus value peaks on that chart, it stays up. That value should be firmly in place and become part of the child. How would maintaining that value be different after it peaks from the 6-year period where you were instilling it? Would it take less effort? Why would skipping any of these affect the ability to implement the next ones?

4. Notice "Releasing" begins at 13 and should be maximized and completed at 18. "Friendship" begins in earnest a few years later at 16 and ideally, would be mature and on a peer-to-peer basis by 21. Notice also that "Obedience" starts to be focused on at birth and should be maximized and in place by three. OK, that's a lot of "noticing" but here are the questions: Why is the order of implementing these so important?

5. How would they build upon one another?

6. Why would switching them cause challenges? For instance, instead of starting to become your child's *friend* at 16, you want to be their friend when they are three or even 10, when *obedience* and *teaching* should be peaking. Why would this cause confusion and counteract the focus that should be in place at that age? Discuss this.

7. Why would instilling *vision* in them need to precede *releasing* them? What happens when permissive parenting allows *releasing* too young, being their *friend* too young and then later tries to bring *obedience?*

    (We recognize most of these concepts haven't been developed yet, so it may be helpful to briefly discuss and revisit these at the end as well)

SEASON II

SUMMER CULTIVATION
(7-12 Years Old)

TEACHING & VISION

During the spring, the little plant has gotten off to a great start and now summer is the season for weeding and feeding. In summer, that is when the farmer applies some fertilizers and the right irrigation—all ingredients that the plant absorbs and integrates into itself to prepare it for a great harvest. This is also the season when the farmer is most diligent to make sure the weeds are kept out. They will choke and stunt the growth of the plant and can either kill it, or seriously diminish the harvest. If you've ever had a garden, you know what I'm talking about. You can get the soil prepared so nicely, get the seed planted and it comes up all looking so promising. But then it seems the weeds just want to take over and you really have to work just to stay ahead of it!

In children's lives, this is the time when they are at the prime season for *Teaching* and *Vision*; the perfect age and season to absorb God's biblical worldview and His vision for the future, taking it into their hearts, minds, and ultimately their lives so that it truly becomes their own. When cultivated into them at the right time, something remarkable happens. Your values and ideas transform to become *their* values and ideas; that is the key! It truly becomes part of who they are—they own it as *their* thinking and *their* plans. Try to do this without first establishing *Obedience* and *Heart*, and it's premature. Do this in the Fall Harvest Season and it's past the optimum time for them to absorb it—but summertime, from about 7-12 is primetime for them to take in the *Teaching* and *Vision*!

It's certainly not as though these things weren't began during the Spring Season—in the same way that some fertilization and weeding happens during the spring in farming. However, the biggest key in the Spring Season is to get the seedbed ready and the seed planted so that the little plant gets going. If that isn't done well, no amount of fertilizing or weeding even applies. Likewise—you have incorporated a base of authority in your child's life and have watched their heart carefully, so that now they are really ready to absorb the *Teaching* and *Vision* of the Summer Cultivation Season. You don't stop the key focuses of the prior season, but since they are now normal, all you do is maintain them and begin to incorporate the priorities of the next season.

In this season, by carefully building into them proper biblical and academic teaching as well as a powerful vision for their future during this Summer Season, then you will be able to maximize the *Encouraging* and *Releasing* of the next Fall Harvest Season when your kids are teens. If you don't build into them a strong biblical worldview coupled with appropriate vision—then when they are teens, they will want to make *their own* vision and worldview, more influenced by culture and friends. Then you won't have the established base to *Encourage* and *Release* them into during the harvest years, and will be doing damage control by trying to convince them of things at a time they aren't as open to it—the wrong season. As you continue through, it should all fit together with greater clarity. So now, let's set out in summer to maximize cultivating the best *Teaching* and *Vision* into your child possible!

CHAPTER 7

TEACHING

N ow is the ideal time to really teach and disciple them. While this certainly began in the earlier years, it is interesting that the world at large seems to understand this season as first grade usually starts at age six or seven. Now, there are preparatory grades like kindergarten and pre-schools, but trying to cram too much teaching into children younger than the Summer Season can detract from the priorities of the Spring Season: *Heart* and *Obedience*. If parents embrace this, it can bring peace and freedom from feeling stressed to teach too soon, as ages 7-12 are the prime time to build into them a strong biblical worldview and is also the prime time to protect them from the devil's worldview of lies.

CHRISTIAN WORLDVIEW

There are two prongs to the teaching value: biblical worldview and academics, and these two are intertwined. We just witnessed the baptism of a young man two weeks ago who is attending a Christian academy that integrates every subject matter with God's Word. He was sharing in his testimony what an impact and transformation this has made on his faith and approach to life. He said something to the effect that since God created everything, naturally, every subject fit within God's Word. For example, he said, since God is a God of order, then math makes sense! I loved that. In our post-Christian atheistic school systems (it's called naturalism, just a nicer sounding term for atheism), we no longer make any connection between God and the sciences, math, literature, art, music or any of it, which is very detrimental.

Sadly, we have forgotten that Jesus has influenced and shaped all of these disciplines. I just read a powerful book called *Person of Interest* by J. Warner Wallace. He was an atheist detective whose wife dragged him to church one Easter. He'd investigated several "nobody, missing person" cases in which there was no crime scene, no physical evidence, and no victim's body. He was intrigued to investigate Jesus' impact in the same way and dove into researching the impact of Jesus on education, science, literature, art, music, religion and culture and realized that if we had no Bible at all— everything contained there could easily be reassembled by how Jesus has impacted all of it. He became a devout believer in Christ from his investigation. So, to think that today we have education divorced from Jesus and God's Word is sad and sinister.

This is why we would propose that particularly in this Spring "teaching" season of elementary school, a Christian worldview is essential to build into their lives and develop their mind and person. It is incomprehensible to imagine an 8- or 9-year-old being taught by a teacher that there is no God and that everything can be explained perfectly by evolution or naturalism. Or that it is a good and normal choice for a child to choose their gender, and we are to honor and celebrate these things; that two dads are just as normal as a dad and a mom. We have lost our minds—but this is quickly becoming the new normal, causing incalculable damage to our children.

A LITTLE HISTORY

Let's cover a brief American History review; I saw you just fall asleep—hang with me, it's just a little over a page! When the Pilgrims landed at Plymouth Rock in 1620, they established Harvard University a mere 16 years later for the *specific purpose* of training pastors for the new commonwealth. It's hard to imagine today, but most of our Ivy League Universities were started for the purpose of training students in God's Word: Harvard, Yale, Princeton, Dartmouth—all started by clergy to train clergy! And this is why Western civilization has led in so many ways as the Word of God formed societies. Oh, how the mighty have fallen! I can remember when I was studying at Oxford University for a brief time and I was in the famed Oxford Bodleian Library. Once again—those well-known universities in England, Oxford, Cambridge—they were started to train people in God's Word! And those were started hundreds of years before our fledgling universities like Yale and Harvard.

I was in that Oxford library and the professor explained that back in the 1200's and for centuries after (We don't know *old* here in America) the outside row of the reading hall beside the windows lining both sides, was reserved for students studying *the important subject*: the Bible. There were a few seats in the center where the light was dimmer for other "lesser" subjects like math or science, but nothing compared to the study of God's Word at university. Obviously, there was no electricity and candles were forbidden in the combustible library, so all they had was the sunlight coming in from the windows, and the best light was of course to be used to study God's Word—The Light!

For hundreds of years after Plymouth Rock here in the "new commonwealth" of America, all of our schools would have taught God's Word as Truth, Genesis as history of creation, opened in prayer, and trained our young people all the subjects from a Christ-centered perspective until the late 1800's when Darwin's theory began to present a "naturalistic" or "atheistic" option for the world as we know it. By 1962, it was made illegal to pray in public schools.

The devil and all his agents have been very effective in removing the Bible, prayer, and God from our schools. And then we seem surprised when there are increased shootings, chaos, and confusion. Lies and confusion are the enemies play-book. Recently here in Florida, there has been a tremendous uproar over legislation that has passed *not* allowing teachers to teach our children that they can choose their gender and sexual orientation. 60 years ago, we passed legislation *not* allowing prayer. Now we have to make laws to stop teachers from telling your 8-year-old boy that he can decide to be a girl and that it's ok if he wants to marry another boy.

Not too long ago these things were illegal and classified in mental health journals as mental illness. When I was born in the 60's, homosexual acts were a *felony* in all 50 states. Think about that for a moment—in my lifetime. Not just taboo—but a felony! Today we celebrate this sin with PRIDE as the unstable ever-changing LGBTQQIPSAA+ movement seeks to swallow up our children. What a slide—from Bible-centered education to sexual and identity chaos on the corner of Sodom and Gomorrah boulevard.

I (Deb) recently sat down with our grandkids to watch a cute cartoon with a family of dogs. Two puppies were playing at a playground and then went to one of their houses and as they opened the front door, two adult dogs were sitting on the couch and the one puppy said, "Hi mommy and mommy." I was stunned! And then saddened that this was in the middle of kid's cartoons. The irony of this example is that actually dogs are *not* confused about this—only people. We have to watch and watch to protect the minds and hearts of our little children.

Don't let society, schoolteachers, and TV shows train your children how to think. As parents, we are responsible to carefully navigate this teaching season with our children in our rapidly declining culture. Any avenues to work together, first in the context of a church family, and then with parents in a co-op to teach them, Christian school options, home-school for some parents, or public schools in the right setting with parental involvement are all options. But we are in a war of major proportions, and you must fight to defend the minds and hearts of your children like never before!

WEED & FEED

In farming, during the spring and summer seasons, there are two elements that you navigate—the feeding: involving fertilizing and irrigation. And weeding: fighting the pests and weeds that desire to overtake and choke out the plants. An offensive and defensive approach! It is no different when you are parenting particularly in this Summer Season. You have to guard very carefully the content of the fertilizer you are putting into your children. Why?

In farming, when you put fertilizer on the plants—it is absorbed by the plant and actually becomes part of the plant itself. Again, this never would happen in the fall season—but the summer is the perfect time. I can remember when in early summer, the corn was up in rows, and I would apply nitrogen fertilizer. It seemed miraculous—you would see the corn plant green up and shoot up almost overnight. It was taking in those nutrients and transferring it to the very body and structure of the crop itself!

Don't miss this point—that is happening to your children! You definitely want to try to make sure they are getting the very best teaching. Good academics in a biblical worldview! Why? Because it is being absorbed into their very mind, heart, and body as they grow, literally becoming who they are, shaping and forming how they think about life and the world as it becomes part of them. There are certainly differing opinions, but to have an openly atheistic teacher or teaching being pumped into my little 7-, 8-, or 9-year-old would be about the worst thing and frankly self-sabotaging thing I could imagine.

FEEDING

Each family has to navigate their academic pathway for their children. The only thing I would encourage is that this season is *the most important time* to ensure that they are getting Christ-centered education. That is less important in the fall—teenage season. For the reasons I said earlier, in the fall the plant isn't absorbing the fertilizer and rain like it is in the summer. A properly prepared teenager is now ready and actually *needs* to learn to navigate the demonic sewage pumped out in the world because they are going to have to know how to handle that—and the high school years, while they are still at home and able to process with their parents is an ideal time. But not in the summer pre-teen years. Let's unpack some of these options:

HOMESCHOOLING

Homeschooling is increasingly accepted in society. It is definitely challenging and certainly not for everyone. There are no shortages of jokes and stereotypes of home school children—and some of them are funny and true! If you want to laugh, look up "Homeschool Family Tim Hawkins" on YouTube. One minute putting all the stereotypes together from the kid's perspective. Here are a few of the lyrics: "We learn about creation, and classic education, we're sponsoring a nation, our homeschool family . . . our parents are the tutors, we build our own computers, we never go to Hooters, our homeschool family . . . our 6-year-old's a surgeon . . ."

Many methods and options are available to help you if you choose this option. Back in Indiana we had another mom who was excellent in writing and loved teaching; she tutored our kids. Look for support and people that can help to fill in areas that are not your strength. Even if you have to pay someone to help you teach your children, it is worth it.

When we moved to Florida our five kids were ages 7-17. One of the advantages of homeschooling is that you can move and not have to worry about new school districts. We moved to four different school systems while our kids were in school. Here in St Cloud Florida, we had an amazing Homeschool CO-OP that consisted of around 30 families and 70 kids. Every Monday, our kids would go there as moms and dads taught subjects they loved and specialized in, both professionally and/or academically. As parents we were just responsible to help make sure the kids did the homework that was assigned throughout the week.

They put together some of the most amazing theatrical productions that our kids got to participate in and it turned out to be a super experience and blessing in our lives. Everyone always seemed concerned about social development for home school kids. You may have known the kids who hide behind Mom or cannot look you in the eye. Regarding that specifically, I (Deb) spent time practicing this at home with my children. I would pretend to be the child and let my child be the adult. I acted out how I wanted my kids to look an adult in the eye and talk loud enough that the adult could easily hear them. In our roleplaying, we added a firm handshake. We practiced this over and over until each of our kids could do this with ease.

These great opportunities at CO-OP as well as deep involvement in church and friends' lives, provided plenty of socialization. Joy Chambers is a mom in our community who decided to put this CO-OP together and lead it. Joy—if you happen to read this, you rock!

Countless options like this exist in communities across the country—or they could be started; families working together. Once you begin to look into it, you will realize that there is unbelievable latitude given in home-education. Another option here in Florida is called Florida Virtual School, which gives the academic class work but allows you to navigate that from a home environment; you can check your area for these opportunities. There is certainly no one-size-fits all, and more than likely, you will utilize various methods throughout your families teaching season.

COVID certainly increased the respect and popularity of homeschooling in the minds of the public. I remember seeing a meme during that time that said, "Perception of Home school moms before COVID" and there was a picture of three homely Amish ladies. Then it said, "Perception of home school moms after COVID" and it was a picture of Wonder Woman.

CHRISTIAN PRIVATE SCHOOL

Christian Private School is certainly another option. A couple advantages of this option is that the education of your children is more in the hands of the school and not as much on the shoulders of mom and dad to direct. Another advantage of a Christian school is that for the most part, the teachers will hold a biblical worldview and hopefully the curriculum is designed to teach all the subjects *integrating God's Word.* That is so important. You really cannot overestimate the power and influence authority figures like teachers have on our moldable little children. When we join teaching all subjects through a biblical lens with teachers who are believers, you have a powerful combination!

Some of the disadvantages of Christian school is that they always seem to want you to pay for these things! So annoying. But don't give up too soon—there are often scholarships and ways to make it work if you keep on asking, seeking, and knocking. Be creative; we've known moms who have worked at the school in an area they liked, allowing all of their children to attend free. Another challenge can be that depending on the model, they may be pushing your kids to be fluent in Latin by age three; that's certainly exaggerated, but both in public and private schools, it is more difficult to control the pace of learning as the whole herd has to go thru together. As we mentioned earlier, we think there are advantages to slowing down the academic pace in the earlier years. There are many opportunities to explore in most communities.

PUBLIC SCHOOLS

For some families, the public-school option is the one for them. Schools are made up of people in specific communities, so every family knows best their own context. Often Charter schools are a form of public education that could have strengths and are popping up everywhere. The biggest key here is that you have to be very engaged. Don't be naïve about the faculty, agenda, or what friends your kids are making. This is true in every setting, but your green-haired, non-binary, they-their pronoun science teacher probably isn't as likely to show up at the Christian school or in your living room. Likewise, the friend who has two mom's or two dad's is becoming more and more common, and these things are extremely complicated, confusing, and controversial. I used to say to our kids, "Show me your friends and I'll show you your future" which is another version of the Bible verse, "Bad company corrupts good character" (1 Cor. 15:33).

Many people argue that we are to be salt and light and it's our job to have our kids winning the world to Christ. My response would be that is the right thing at the wrong time. The Summer Teaching Season is not the best time for your child to be confronting godless demonic deceptions that come through teachers and peers. This is the time where they are absorbing and for you to diligently protect what is going into them. The season for them to defend their faith and confront the darkness is coming and very soon—Fall! But not now. Now is the time for you to carefully develop that world-view conviction in them so that they are fully equipped to navigate and defend a biblical worldview in a secular culture.

If this is done in the proper order, it can be the most beautiful thing to see your 16- and 17-year-old debating and defending the Truth in their schools and environments. I remember our daughter at probably 17 was taking a dual enrollment art course at our Community College and she came home telling me they had a naked man posing in front of the class they were drawing. What on earth#%@!?! Some things I can't even imagine. But the difference was that she was now in a season where she was maturing, and we could talk through various things. Today, she is a licensed Christian mental health counselor probably helping people work through having to draw naked men in college.

A pastor I used to have would always say, "If Satan can't stop you, he'll stampede you." And this really applies to this entire "seasons of parenting" concept. Satan knows you care about the right things for your children and he's not able to stop you—so instead, he'll push you to get in a hurry and jump ahead to the next season too soon. Either way it is detrimental. The right thing at the wrong time is the wrong thing. There are even entire ministries built around getting kids to lead church movements and evangelistic campaigns, and while it is right and good to build into our kids the Word of God—what this whole thing is about—when you give a kid, particularly in this Summer Season from 7-12, too much spiritual authority, responsibility, and spot-light, it often does not age well.

Public school may be the option you choose but be involved and aware of what they are getting taught. I would go to the greatest extent possible to know their teachers, being involved and making sure you keep communication very open; again, these apply in all settings but especially if you have your kids in a public secular school environment. It's really hard to wrap your head around just how rapidly our cultures values have deteriorated where evil is called good and good is seen as evil and hatred (Isaiah 5:20). If you had to make the choice between public school for elementary ages or high school, we would choose high school. Most public schools encourage parent-teacher communication easily through a forum they provide. Take full advantage of it.

What we see happen more often is that parents didn't pay attention to the *Heart* and *Obedience* focus of the Spring Season, left the kids get all kinds of godless education and friends during the Summer *Teaching* and *Vision* Season, and then during the Fall Harvest Season, those teenage years when the fruit is now coming out and concerning the parent, then they will pull them out of public education and try to get them into a Christian School environment to fix them. Often the ideal time for that was the prior season and now your teen is not open or receptive any more.

Back to our farming metaphor, you can go out into the field in the fall, when the crop is going into seed, and put all kinds of the best fertilizer on the ground or water the soil until it's soaked—but the plant isn't absorbing it anymore. That was the spring and summer Season. Now, all I can do as a farmer is navigate the harvest—seeking to do the best I can to make sure the crop is released in the best way. All analogies break down, and there is no doubt that teens are still absorbing and learning, but parents of any teens will agree that it is different. They are not as open to your input. Put all your focus on doing the right thing in the season you are in. The next season will be here soon enough!

BIBLICAL FEEDING

We said at the beginning, the *Teaching* value during this Summer Season involves two aspects: Academic and Biblical worldview teaching. Certainly, our discussion of different schooling options took care of the academic aspect of teaching, and in varying degrees incorporated the biblical feeding. I want to take some time here to specifically discuss how you can ensure that your child—who is now in that prime season to build a biblical foundation, can do that to the best degree.

SUNDAY SCHOOL

Hand in hand with the value of engaging in a church family is having your children be involved as well. Hopefully your church has some form of Sunday School with concentrated Bible teaching for the kids to be involved in. I was just talking with our son yesterday; he and his wife run our churches kid's ministry and we were discussing the balance between solid Bible content and having fun. We discussed that particularly in the 1st thru 5th grade classes—which ironically is right around 6-10 years old, this summer "teaching" season, the kids are at the prime age where they are really absorbing God's Word.

However, if it is the most boring thing they've ever experienced, it's probably not sticking.

I once heard someone tell preachers about preaching, "If you don't strike oil within the first 30 minutes, stop boring." Well, I think that's even more true for kids. There is an interesting balance between fun and Bible. You want them to recall their experience with positive feelings so that they are open to receiving the content. On the other hand, if it's just fun with very little Bible, then what have we really accomplished that's shaping their mind and heart?

Also, this is a good time to engage your kids through the week on what they learned. If your church sends crafts or papers home with your kids, don't miss the opportunity to talk with them about what they learned and continue to build upon that lesson. This is the season—if you don't do it now, it's not likely they will be bringing papers home from Sunday School wanting to talk with you about them when they are 17. There are other great programs to fill your kids time and minds—AWANA is still an excellent option as well as finding a good Vacation Bible School for your kids to have both fun and Bible together. I've known parents who will send their kids to three VBS's during the summer—Vacation Bible School for kids, just vacation for parents—both probably needed!

DINNER TIME

Speaking of God-conversations about papers your kids bring home from Sunday school, one of the best opportunities a family has to get together is by planning and guarding a dinner hour where everyone comes together around the table. I know, it's difficult in our fast food, digital age, but that makes it even *more* important to plan and protect. Have everyone set aside their phones, games, and iPads and take the time to see how everyone is really doing. We recommend having a "Device Drop" box where everything goes in. That time is a really strategic time to find out how the day went, noticing if someone is particularly quiet or upset, sharing highs and lows of the day.

The subject of Bible devotions can be challenging but taking a few minutes around the dinner table to read a verse or two and talk about it can be very positive, and 5 or 10 minutes goes a long way; remember the "stop boring" part earlier.

BEDTIME

And while we are on the subject of devotions, bedtime is another great time for reading good Bible stories or character-building books to your kids. Mid to late Spring and Summer are the very best times to do this. Most often, your teenagers aren't asking you to read bedtime stories, but your eight-years-old is open to absorbing that. I know bedtime can get quite frustrating to parents. We are exhausted from the day, we've done homework, made dinner and now all we can think about is going to bed—or at least getting the kids to bed! But this is a pivotal moment at a critical season. Please seriously consider trying different methods of bedtime routines until you find something that you are willing to do because this is the absolute best time of day for your kids to tell you something they have wanted to tell you all day. Maybe you noticed one of the kids was "off" a bit at dinner time, make a mental note of that and perhaps spend a little extra time before bed trying to sense what is going on in their heart, asking how they are doing. Please parent, do not skimp on this area of parenting. If you can somehow anticipate it—perhaps rest earlier in the day to prepare for this 30-minute time of day, you will never regret it.

Kids are talkative and more open at bedtime than most other times of the day. I know, sometimes it's just to delay having to go to sleep.

We were just talking with one of our kids about this the other day and they were saying just what we described—they are tired and, in a hurry, and that's when the kids want to talk and talk . . . and talk. So, they have recently made a decision to intentionally start bedtime a half hour earlier, that way they have more time built in and everyone isn't feeling as rushed. That has made a big difference.

GOOD DIGITAL CONTENT

Finding good, engaging things for your kids to listen to is powerful. Our kids practically memorized the Focus on the Family Adventures in Odyssey series. These were stories where God's Word and qualities were incorporated in engaging ways—or adventures! These were back in the days of cassette tapes, and our kids would listen to them while they were going to sleep, or while they were coloring, playing, or doing chores around the house. This was just one way to pump into their little minds Truth, wisdom, and character almost automatically.

I'll never forget when one of our kids went off to college one of the first nights, he asked his roommate if he has ever heard of "Adventures in Odyssey?" His roommate said "Yes, I love them." So, they started listening to them at night! And this wasn't the same one who asked us to keep the cassettes for when he grew up! Just imagine. This is a powerful example of how these things, when fertilized at the right time, become normal later and are deeply valued even two seasons later. Try to introduce something like that for the first time to your college student and you couldn't pay enough to get them to do it.

Super tools for cultivating biblical teaching into your kids during this Summer Season are:

- Adventures in Odyssey
- Super Book
- The Greatest Adventures—Stories from the Bible
- Story Keepers
- Stories of the Bible (YouTube)
- Listener Kids (YouTube)
- New City Catechism
- Uncle Arthur's Bedtime Stories

We mentioned many of these back in the Spring Season, but they should be full tilt, peddle down all through the Summer Season. Maximizing a combination of all of these, will enable you to fill their growing sponge minds with God's Word and God's worldview at the critical time in their lives when their thoughts and personality are being formed. They are more open to receive it than they ever will be. It is the perfect season!

Our teenage boys loved watching Shark Tank. One of the products on there was called Scrub Daddy. It was a sponge that when it was in warm water, was soft and absorbent like a normal sponge, soaking up water easily. But when it is put under cold water, it becomes stiff and hard—for scrubbing, but not for absorbing. I actually just went on Amazon and ordered a pack. Ugg, too easy!

That is a pretty good analogy of your kids—during this summer season, their minds are like the Scrub Daddy in warm water; they are absorbing everything that hits them. Then, when they are teenagers, during the Fall Harvest Season, it's like the Scrub Daddy under cold water—where it becomes hard and abrasive, better for scrubbing than absorbing. Both have their purpose, but they are different. Be sure to maximize this season for putting Truth and God's Word into your kid's soft sponge minds now, before the cold water hits them!

———

KID DATES

This season is the prime time to be prioritizing Daddy-daughter/son dates. Maybe you call that Date Daddy. While the Teaching focus begins in the Spring Season, probably around three, particularly in this Summer Season, you have a powerful impact on your kids when you take them out and spend one-on-one time with them. I can remember taking my girls to Richards Restaurant when we lived in Indiana. They had a toy basket and the kids always got to get some little prize when we left. Sitting there with my 7-year-old daughter having breakfast was a great time for relationship and conversation. Now, it's not like this was some heavy Bible-study. Sometimes we'd just play Hangman on the back of the placemat. Now that I *am* thinking about this, it does make me wonder. Playing Hangman just a few years after we sang "Rockabye Baby in the treetop, when the wind blows . . . down will come baby, cradle and all. Now go to sleep honey." You really do kind of marvel how any of it works out?

But anyhow, those were great times to build trust, talk about little things in life, and open up the way so that when my daughters were 17, we were still going out and working through things like CS Lewis' Screwtape Letters, where he talks about how the devil tempts us and tries to deceive us; or friend and relationship issues. Building the pattern at seven opens the way to help them navigate the harvest season at 17.

I've focused on the girls—the same is true for the boys. They all enjoy that one-on-one time in whatever setting you build it in. For my boys, I did the same thing. Motorcycle rides were super fun. Dates can be as simple as a walk in the neighborhood or sitting alone with one child on the swing at night just watching the stars. It doesn't have to cost money, it's the time spent with the child that matters. And dates like this were of course true for Mom as well, but I believe, if Dad is in the family, him taking the initiative to spend that one-on-one time is extra critical and impacting. These are the activities that cultivate open hearts to receive the good fertilizer of God's Word and awareness of the growing weeds, which is the next subject.

WEEDING

I want to close this *Teaching* portion on the defensive side: Weeding. As I mentioned at the beginning, in the summer the farmer has two main objectives: feeding; involving fertilizing and irrigation. And weeding; fighting the pests and weeds that desire to overtake and choke out the plants. Here I want to specifically zero in on how to keep the weeds and pests away from your child so that they aren't choked in their development.

TECHNOLOGY

Not surprising, technology tops the list of things to watch out for. Why? We are all facing a challenge that has never existed in the history of the world until well, about 20 years ago. What is that? Practically all knowledge and content at my fingertips all the time! Think about that for a moment. Right now, I'm thinking about some obscure question like, "When is George Washington's birthday?" Now, maybe you just know stuff like that—but I'm guessing already you've either done it or know what you would do, exactly what I just did: take your phone out and say, "When is George Washington's Birthday?" And in far less time than it's taken me to type this "February 22, 1732" comes up along with his picture and a link to anything else you'd ever imagine knowing about George Washington.

Now, on one hand this is a real blessing—carrying around a whole library in your pocket with your own personal librarian Siri there to help you find anything you want. But then there is the dark side; what your children would *not* have had access to until they were in college or grown, they can now get at age seven in a smart device. The most vile, evil stuff we may not even have imagined is available to your children in written, graphic, and video content *in about three clicks at all times!!* As parents we have to be vigilant to guide and guard this complex challenging new world!

Having a phone is not a right for your kids—and *you* get to decide when that happens. For us, it was a little easier, because our kids were just entering the teen years when cell phones and smart phones were becoming normal, so it was pretty easy for us to say, "You get a phone when you start driving." It seemed reasonable that if they are responsible enough to handle a 3-4,000-pound machine that can kill people, (yes, I just typed in "how much does a car weigh?) they are probably ready to handle their own phone. Another dad said he will require their kids to have a job before they get a phone. Today if you make these rules, you will face a whole lot of pressure, but parents *you decide* and don't let the pressure of society make your family decisions.

FILTERS

Utilizing filters for your home Wi-Fi system, always making sure your kids know you have their passwords and are looking—and be looking! —all of this is helpful. But don't kid yourself, none of it is foolproof. How many of us as parents have been watching a video on our phone and when it is over another one pops up and starts, and then another, and another. At times, a video will pop up that you wouldn't

SEASONS OF PARENTING

have chosen. Well, if it happens to us, it happens to our kids. We need to be their protectors and very attentive to what they are watching.

Filters are helpful but spend a few minutes trying to get around them and see how effective they really are—your kids will. We have used various filters. I remember when we had Covenant Eyes, which helps to guard what we watch. They had an app on your phone with a big eyeball that you would click on to do your internet searches, and then it would flag content. The part I couldn't figure out was that my Safari App was still there as well. I thought, "Wait a minute—so if I have the integrity to choose to go in through the big eyeball, I'll be watched, but if I choose the Safari internet search app, then there is no filter?" I talked to a rep about that, and they said, "Yea, that's a weakness." I thought, oh my! It was not really helpful. If the child wants to get around it, they will.

One of the better accountability systems is xxxchurch.com. It's not actually a filter, but it sends content reports to selected people about where you have been on the devices. I find that this is about as effective as anything for accountability and could be a good help and deterrent for your children as well.

Talk with other families and friends to learn what others are doing; find people who are computer savvy to help you set things up. Paying careful attention to the digital lives of your kids is so important. Our little kids have access to so many devices with content we couldn't have imagined—and still may not! If kids get enticed and get a taste for the wrong things, it can open all kinds of doors to Satan and get them on a path to harmful addictions. Pray for the Lord's wisdom and protection in this. He knows everything that is going on and we definitely need His direction in this area.

You've probably heard the saying, "The best defense is a good offense" and this is true here as well. By carefully applying these principles in their right season—an offensive strategy, you help to overpower the lies and sewage the enemy is peddling all around us. A good book on navigating technology is *The Tech-wise Family* by Andy and Amy Crouch.

FRIENDS

Pay special attention to your kid's friends, and particularly in the pre-teen, summer years, guard where they go and who they go with. Too much stuff happens in unguarded settings and so parents, pay attention who your child is playing with and what houses they stay at. We have a 2-story home with bedrooms upstairs, so when the children are at our house, our standard is that the kids play downstairs. The upstairs is for sleeping not playing. When we have youth parties or Bible studies, kids are not allowed upstairs. Being aware of where they are can help head off a lot of problems.

This is the season to really control your kid's friends—and you can. If you see behavior in one of your children's friends that you do not like, it is just a matter of a few days or weeks that most likely your child will be acting the same way. Beware of peer pressure. The saying, "One rotten apple spoils the whole bunch" isn't famous for nothing. The Bible simply says it this way, "Bad company corrupts good character." 1 Cor. 15:33 You have much less control of their friend choices during the Fall Harvest Season; this is OK, and actually healthy. If you watch and cultivate their input diligently and carefully now, it will more naturally take care of itself in the next season.

QUESTIONS FOR DISCUSSION

1. Why is it important to teach a biblical foundation and worldview while children are in this Summer Season?

2. What are some new thoughts or insights you picked up around the discussion of the various schooling options presented? What is the best schooling option for your family? What are the challenges?

3. Maximizing digital content for biblical and character building is an important strategy. Of the options presented here, what have you used and what others might you try? Where could you be more intentional about replacing secular "programming" with intentional biblical input?

4. How important do you see having a family dinner time being? What are the challenges to making this happen?

5. How can you make your bedtime routine more intentional for biblical and character building?

6. What are some ideas for parent-child dates that you do or might add to your family life?

7. What type of filters or device monitoring do you have in place for your children? When should your children be given their own phone or other devices? Are you checking on them?

8. In what ways do you see friends influencing your kids positively and negatively? Are there examples that come to mind where you should change that for your children?

CHAPTER 8

A DISCIPLESHIP PLAN

D uring the second half of the Summer Season, this is a great time to put in place a specific discipleship plan that culminates in a rite of passage as they enter into the Fall Harvest Season! You'll notice on the Changing Seasons Chart (Appendix B) that is right when the *Teaching* focus peaks, and this is the culmination of their discipleship plan. The *Man of the Sword* and the *Princess of the Rings* 2-year discipleship plans are examples that culminate in an impacting ceremony at 13 that fills them with empowerment and confidence launching into their teenage years.

MAN OF THE SWORD

Deb and I had found these Teen Bibles in magazine form that were fun for kids. We first found the *New Testament Refuel: The Complete New Testament for Guys (Biblezeens)* and it had sections titled "Man of the Sword—how unstoppable warriors got so awesome." We also got the companion version *Refuel: Epic Battles of the Old Testament* which had the same "Man of the Sword" articles from the Old Testament. As of this writing, they were both still available on Amazon. I got both of these for my boys when they were around 11 and we put together a 2-year plan where they would read these and then do a character study around each of these Bible personalities. They thought it was cool having a magazine style Bible designed for them!

The study was called a "Man of the SWORD study." And I broke down S.W.O.R.D. into Servanthood, Wisdom, Obedience, Respect, and Determination. They would read these "Man of the Sword" inserts that had a Bible character and a corresponding Bible passage that talked about them. We had our boys read that, then read the Bible passage and do a report on that person.

The reports consisted of putting into their own words all of those different S.W.O.R.D. qualities that they noticed from the "Man of the Sword" character in the Bible. Between the Old and New Testaments, there were around 50 of them. In some cases, the magazine duplicated a character, so I picked a different one from the Bible. We took two years to do that, so it averaged about one every other week. They would write out the study for the character in their notebook and then we would go out together and talk about it.

At the end of this we had a "Man of the Sword Final Thesis." Sounds like big stuff—and it was a big project for a 12-year-old. We took extra time and I edited it so that the spelling was correct. They typed it and we put a special book report cover on it—made it look super important and official. It was a big accomplishment, and they were proud of it.

RITE OF PASSAGE CEREMONY

Once they had completed this study, it culminated in a "Man of the SWORD Ceremony" on their 13th birthday. This was the night they would be presented with their shining, glistening sword! Justin got Peter's sword from Chronicles of Narnia and Micah got the Sword of Solomon. When the big night came, I put on my best suit and our son had a nice 3-piece suit and tie on.

When everyone arrived, probably 70 people or so, we had a combination of video, when Peter was given the sword from the Chronicles of Narnia movie, a battle scene and discussion of the battle we are in. For Micah, we found a movie of Solomon and played the part where he asked for wisdom, and then the scene where he demonstrated his wisdom with the two moms' arguing over the child. And we showed a final scene of the Temple and the Ark of the Covenant—which was carved in the handle of his sword, and how that pointed ahead to the Gospel. Today with YouTube, these clips are easy to find.

We shared the work they had done over the past 2-½ years and showed the gathered group the "Final Thesis" really highlighting the quality and amount of work that took. Then for each of the boys we chose four godly men to take a couple minutes to speak into their lives, challenging, empowering, and blessing them. After this, I presented them with their own personally imprinted "Sword of the Spirit" which is the Word of God. I then pulled out their own gleaming real sword with the SWORD qualities imprinted on the blade and gave it to them.

Then as they knelt, clutched their new Bible in one hand and their new glistening sword in the other, the four men who had spoken into them and I laid our hands on his head in a holy moment of empowerment and passage from boyhood to manhood. We prayed over him calling on God to fulfill His purpose in this new man's life. My eyes are leaking right now typing this out.

After this I took his sword and "Knighted" him, dubbing him a "Man of the Sword." It was kind of cool because at Micah's ceremony, now Justin was 15, so he brought his sword in, and I used Micah's and Justin used his own sword and we crossed them over on his head as he was "Knighted."

THE VALUE OF CEREMONY

Here is something to think about. We have really lost much in the value of ceremony in our contemporary culture. Churches used to be very liturgical, weddings formal and filled with ceremony and institutions had many formal codes. For years now, everything has moved to more and more casual, and while I'm not complaining about not having to wear a suit and tie to church because I like casual—what it does is actually *elevates* the importance and value of ceremony all the more. Something that is less common is even more impactful. So, to make a big deal about your young man crossing from boyhood to manhood is empowering as you are calling things that are not as though they are (Rom 4:17).

Now they are entering their budding manhood with a charge, an identity, a blessing, and a path to run forward on—all empowering things as they enter this Fall Harvest Season with hope, confidence, and clarity. One book that I have found very valuable is *Raising a Modern-Day Knight: A Father's Role in Guiding His Son to Authentic Manhood* by Robert Lewis.

For centuries, orthodox Jews have practiced a coming-of-age ceremony called a Bar Mitzvah; a ceremony at 13 years of age that marks the time when a boy or girl becomes a Jewish adult. Sadly, this is missing in our western culture where children too often stumble and feel their way into adulthood like the 3-blind mice. But we can change this. No one gave us any real roadmap for these things, so we were just grabbing and picking things up as we went. Hopefully, some of these suggestions give you ideas to either utilize or encourage your own quest to intentionally disciple your children. There is no one plan that fits everyone—but I do believe the concepts of empowering, blessing, and acknowledging that they are now transitioning into adulthood is what would be helpful for all parents to give to their children as they enter their teen years.

PRINCESS OF THE RINGS

The focus of what we did with our three daughters was trying to give them a vision and the value of a heart for God and purity during their teenage years. Part of this involved a promise ring with intentional symbols that would signify both their commitment to the Lord and their commitment to keep themselves pure for a day when they would potentially find a husband. This ring became a highlight of their 13th ceremony. When they were 12, I took them shopping for their special ring, and this wasn't just some bubble-gum ring, we went to a real live jewelry store and together looked at them and talked about symbolism and what it could mean for different rings. Then I put together a personalized plaque with their baby picture and a current picture as well as a commitment in their own words that we worked up together. On their 13th birthday, Deb and I took our daughter and went out on a special date to a nice restaurant that she chose and gave her the promise ring and special plaque. So, for our girls, that was the ceremony; private and personal but very meaningful.

Thomas Todd, who has been a committed co-laborer in our church for many years, was involved with our boys and these Man of the Sword ceremonies and he adapted it for his girls as "Princess of the Rings" with a discipleship plan. He developed the acronym R.I.N.G.S. in similar fashion. A Princess of the RINGS is: Resolute, Insightful, Noble, Godly, and Submissive. He utilized similar studies for women in the Bible studying those character qualities and had his daughter put together a report and gave her a Promise Ring.

LESSONS LEARNED

I asked Thomas if he would do this again and plans to implement this with his younger girls when they are that age. He said he will, but with one adjustment. He will be more involved with them when they are doing their studies, working through it together. I agree with that as I think back with my boys—they pretty much did their "Man of the Sword" studies on their own, then we would meet and talk about them. In retrospect, I think it would have been helpful to spend more time with them working through it together.

Another lesson we have learned in discussing with our grown children is that we focused a lot on "character qualities." While part of the study was to highlight both where they did and did not demonstrate them, the emphasis that was perceived was this high moral standard without adequate discussion about what happens when that isn't met. The truth is, we all miss the mark; we all sin. If I were doing it today, I would incorporate in each character study where they sinned and how God forgave and used them in spite of their sin. Then tie that into the whole purpose of the Gospel, and why Jesus, the only "perfect man" came to pay it all.

The Bible highlights very human and real men and women who failed badly, but God used greatly; Moses murdered a man, David also was a murderer and adulterer—Paul was too for that matter. Solomon, while the wisest man alive, lost his wisdom and went against nearly everything God said about accumulating chariots, gold, and wives. That is why we needed and need Jesus, and points to a relationship with Him based on grace.

By looking more intentionally at both the victories and sins in these Bible characters, and tying it into the gospel, I think that would have encouraged more honest discussion about what was going on in their own lives at the time, and how to get back on track as we fight life's real battles with the Sword of the Spirit. So, that is hindsight that may help you do it better with your own kids.

Hopefully these examples give you something to build from. There is certainly no one-size-fits-all. Dozens of approaches could be taken. We had big misses and gaps in our efforts, but God still used it. Since simply *having* an intentional plan to disciple and develop your children is largely absent today, anything you intentionally design to disciple and then celebrate their transition from childhood to manhood and womanhood is priceless.

If your life is extremely difficult and you are barely making it from day to day, or this feels overwhelming, just recognize that any intentional effort is better than nothing. Spending time watching movies together created with godly values in them or intentionally picking some books that you could read together that will help inspire your soon-to-be teen to live with godly vision will be helpful.

Also, don't be afraid to enlist the help of other friends, mentors, or pastors to help put these things together as well. This might seem overwhelming, but we have included a lot of resources in Appendix C at the end of the book. In that appendix, we have included details of what the studies included, the ceremony, and even sample invitations that we sent out for the ceremony. While you are certainly welcome to use any or all of it, the intention is not that you would copy these things exactly, but that they would provide a springboard for you to work from and build something for your own situation.

LAYING THE TRACK

None of this is perfect or always works out according to the ideal plan. Life is messy and each child is different, but that should still not be a reason to abandon a plan. That's a bit like saying that because trains sometimes go off the tracks, tracks are unnecessary, and we are going to stop having tracks for trains. No, of course not. We live in a fallen world with many challenges, and a real enemy. Having a discipleship plan that you lovingly and carefully implement, helps to cultivate God's Word into their hearts and lives during a critical season in their lives. As they live it out in their teen-years you celebrate and encourage. When they get off track, you demonstrate redemption, forgiveness and getting back on track by pointing them to Jesus. The beauty of *Teaching* and the upcoming *Vision* that we will cover next, is that you have a track that both you and your kids know and embrace. Intentional and loving discipleship plans along with ceremony are invaluable, no matter how unqualified we can often feel as parents.

If you have raised one child through the teen years and it isn't going well and you have been through disappointments with them, don't give up! We have watched loving, careful and intentional parents try so hard to raise a child up to be a godly adult that will walk closely with the Lord, but then the teen years hit, and things start to come off the rails and they start making choices that the parents don't approve of. Soon life is full of fights, disappointments, and a child that is growing up walking away from the Lord and all they have taught them.

At that point, parents can throw up their hands and say, "What's the use of trying?" and stop intentionally investing in the younger kids. Don't give up. Hang in there and keep doing the things you know are helpful to invest in your younger children. The story isn't finished yet. Don't let the choices and decisions of the older child take away the opportunity for your younger children to go through these discipleship plans. Each child is wired differently, and what can look like freedom to an older child on the front end, often comes with painful consequences on the back end, and all of the younger children are watching all of it. It is still worth it, and each child deserves your best attention.

QUESTIONS FOR DISCUSSION

1. Why would it be helpful to have an intentional discipleship plan?

2. What does the S.W.O.R.D. stand for in the Man of the Sword?

3. What does R.I.N.G.S. stand for in the Princess of the Rings?

4. What are some reasons that having a formal ceremony could be helpful as your child transitions from boyhood to manhood?

5. What specific resources and suggestions are provided here to help you put your plan together? How can you customize your own plan?

CHAPTER 9

VISION

This Summer Season is the time to specifically cultivate *Vision* into your pre-teen's life. Proverbs famously states, "Where there is no vision, the people perish." The ESV states "Where there is no prophetic vision the people cast off restraint." (Prov. 29:18 ESV) That verse is especially applicable here. When is the stereotypical time that kids "cast off restraint?" Sure—those teenage years! Oh, the dread that is often expressed. That's the season when biology and society can both collide drawing teens into all kinds of "restraint-less" activities. But, as parents, if we are intentional and planning for it, we have the season before the teenage years to place in our kids a vision for what we would like their desired future to hold. The perfect time to do this is during this Summer Cultivation Season, before those often-turbulent teenage years hit. But that is not when you are naturally thinking about doing it. When you place this vision in your child, starting slowly at the beginning of summer around seven and peaking at 13, he is wide open to it. (Refer back to the Season Change Chart in Appendix B) He embraces you and the vision you are sharing. Remember, he still thinks you are cool and amazing and really values what you are saying.

VISION AS FERTILIZER

In our farming metaphor, like we mentioned with teaching, vision too is like fertilizer. The fertilizer provides specific ingredients that the plant needs which later comes out in a better harvest. However, that has to be applied at the right time. I remember when I used to farm, we would apply nitrogen to our corn during the summer when the corn was probably 12-15" tall. I would drive the tractor with the applicator up and down the rows and the nitrogen would be placed in the ground near the corn and you could almost see the corn grow and get greener. There was a marked difference between places that the nitrogen was applied and where it wasn't; in the skipped places, the corn was smaller and less productive. What happened? Well, it was just the right time where that corn plant absorbed the fertilizer, took it in, and it actually became part of the plant affecting the seed that would come off in harvest.

But here is the huge point! If I would have waited to go out in that field in the fall, during the harvest season when the plant is almost full-grown and then I would have applied the nitrogen, it would have done absolutely *no* good! Why? Because the corn plant is not in the place where it is absorbing fertilizer now, it is ready for harvest. So, notice the major difference—in the Summer Season, the corn completely absorbs it, and the fertilizer becomes part of the plant. In the Fall Season, it absorbs none of it and has no effect.

Now, let's take this example and compare it to vision in our kids. Up ahead, we have multiple chapters each highlighting a different vision piece, but let's just take one quick example to show what we are talking about: the importance of working and getting a job. If you are fertilizing that vision into your child's life when she is 10 or 11, what does she think about that? It sounds awesome! You tell your daughter, "Now sweetheart, guess what? When you are 16 and you have your driver's license you will go out and get a job at McDonalds (or any entry-level job). That will be amazing because they give you your very own uniform and you get to make your own money which will allow you to buy your own stuff!" What do they think about that? *Wow! Amazing!* It sounds great—they don't really understand it, but at this stage, they are more pliable and open to embracing the vision you are cultivating into their lives. You are speaking this vision and destiny into their lives at just the right time. And the most powerful part is if it is done now, what started as your vision absorbs and transforms into *their vision*. That is the critical distinction.

Suppose on the other hand, you have never talked about this, and you now have a teenager that is totally absorbed in videogames and friends. Of course, he always wants to do stuff that takes money and you have been dishing dollars out like you're the government and then at say 17 you are fed up and you sit him down and say the same exact thing; something like, "Now son, you need to go get a job at McDonalds. That will be amazing because they give you your very own uniform and you get to make your own money . . ." Interestingly, at this stage it doesn't sound nearly as great. He is more shocked and resistant than open and receptive. They have ripened and they are much more interested in things that seem fun or easier. Somehow, getting up early and getting a job doesn't have nearly the appeal at 17 as it does at 10!

However, if you have carefully cultivated that vision into them earlier and they have absorbed it, then when they get into that fall teenage season, it is part of who they are; it has become *their vision not yours*, they own it and embrace it. *That is the key difference!* Then, during the fall harvest season, you are not trying to put that vision into them, you are merely *Encouraging* and *Releasing* that vision out of them—they want to do it and just need your help stewarding the harvest! They have been planning on and anticipating these things for years. You aren't the obstacle; you are their ally trying to help them over the normal obstacles of life; a monumental difference!

THE RIGHT AMOUNT

When you think of *Vision* as fertilizer, something important to keep in mind is that the right amount of fertilizer causes the plant to absorb it, take it in and it becomes part of the plant. Too much however, will burn and actually kill the plant. This is true of vision as well. Because you are sprinkling these things into your kid's lives before they are actually really thinking about it or utilizing it, you have to be careful not to overdo it. All of the upcoming *Vision* subjects are things sprinkled into their lives in the right amount over a few years time; in our zeal to make sure they get it, we can overdo it and choke them out. If you say too much at one time, they can feel overwhelmed rather than excited.

A couple memories come to mind. I remember talking to one of our younger children about college and mentioned the detail of moving away from home and living with friends. Immediately they expressed fear at the thought of moving away from home. So, that was our cue to talk at this point in broader terms, without getting into the details too quickly; that will come. Another funny example is about marriage. Several of our kids when we talked to them about getting married would announce they were going to marry me or Daddy. That is who they love more than anyone at that time, so don't push the issue. I remember saying, "Well, I'm already married to Daddy, but let's not worry about it right now. Mommy is always going to love you. When you get older, I bet you won't really want to marry me, let's just wait and see!" I was careful not to demean him or his idea because those were his true feelings at that time.

Another truth about fertilizer is that if you are careful to apply it every year to the soil, it has an accumulative effect and continues to enrich the soil for the future crop. This is also true of vision in your family—all of these things will become part of your family culture, so that what you have shared and instilled as vision into the older kids, gets more naturally absorbed in the younger ones.

HAPPENS AUTOMATICALLY?

Someone may think that this "vision" just happens automatically, and that is true, to an extent. Part of that depends upon the culture of the family and what they have done. For instance, where I grew up in Indiana, everybody I knew got their driver's license at 16 years old—and I'm not talking about 16 ½. I mean on your birthday you were in the license branch taking the test! Now, you may be waiting there until you are 16 ½ before they call your number. Did my dad sit down with me at 10 years old and say, "Son, when you are 16, you can look forward to getting your driver's license and that will give you freedom to go where you want and . . ." No, he sure didn't. It was our culture; everybody did that! All my friends, all my siblings, it was just normal.

However, when Deb and I and our five kids moved to Florida our kids were 7-17 years old. There was a completely different culture surrounding the subject of getting a driver's license. Kids were turning 16 and many it seemed had never even thought about that yet. Kids well past driving age couldn't get jobs because they couldn't drive and somehow just now started to think about it! So, depending on what your background has been, it pays to think through these various issues and intentionally decide what you want them to do, rather than just leave it to what naturally happens. Because, in case you haven't looked lately, what naturally happens with teens is too often they get into alcohol, or drugs, they get into relationships and pregnancies, or they won't get out and get jobs and be responsible. That is what too often naturally happens.

We watched many families not building in a plan or any vision. The kids were pretty good as preteens, then as they were getting old enough to start working and having responsibilities the teens just stayed like a child. Some would not even go to school during high school. Their parents would coax, bribe, scream, and physically try to get them out of bed. The part that was missing was *any meaningful vision for the future*, so why go to school? Why do any homework? They had no future thoughts, and so as their minds and bodies grew, they became more and more inward, lazy and visionless.

So, we don't want to just leave to chance this *Vision* piece. While you may naturally get some of these things right—like driver's license in my case. There are others you may not think about during that Summer Cultivation Season, and then during the teen season, when they are not absorbing your vision nearly as well anymore, you just pray and hold your breath! Things like how they are going to approach relationships with the opposite sex, getting a job, living life on mission, going to college, moving out on their own, among other things. These are all positive vision pieces you want to cultivate into your pre-teen's life.

But there are also negatives that you also want to give your child a vision about. If you wait until your 17-year-old comes home smelling like alcohol to discuss those dangers, again, he is probably not in the "absorbing your vision" place. He's absorbing the alcohol. But if you would have had meaningful conversations about why he should stay away from this, and how to respond when his friends want him to participate when he was 8-11, he would have probably been very open to this, and absorbed that vision into his life so that when he is faced with it at 17, he has been prepped and embraced this ideal. The same is true for smoking, sex and dating, drugs, gambling, pornography and the like.

PRODUCT GUARANTEE

So, you may be thinking, "Great—so you mean I just talk about these things before they are teenagers, and then they are just going to want to do them all like little angels or robots. Right?" Not exactly. There's no guarantee. These are people, not coffee pots. With the prevalence of all of these things in society, it is quite likely that they will get into some of them. Having a strong emphasis on the Gospel and open communication helps to navigate through these challenges.

Back to the train-track metaphor, I view this *Vision* like laying tracks down for your children. By putting in place the parallel rails of mission and vision for your preteens to see clearly and run on as they go through their teenage years, there is a much better potential that they *will* run on it. The Bible even speaks of a Train and the importance of laying a track. You may be familiar with it. "TRAIN up a child in the way he should go, and when he is old, he will not depart from it." Proverbs 22:6 What is Solomon saying here about this train? Basically, if you lay a track for them, "the way he should go" then when he is old, or going into adulthood, they won't depart from the track.

When you have given a prescribed rail to run on or show clearly the vision for the way he should go, now that track is in place to roll forward on and you can just help push them down the track. They are excited about going on mission trips during their middle school years. They have jobs they are encouraged to get as soon as they are able, which gives them a sense of accomplishment. They are anticipating getting their driver's license. They are working towards buying a car.

They are preparing to go on a 3-month mission trip during their 16th year, which is a *big* deal and stretches their faith (as well as Dad and Mom's), they are clear on how they are navigating the girlfriend/boyfriend situation.

All of these are tracks that have been laid down for them so that as they are in the Harvest Season, they have the rails of a clear vision to sequentially run on. Many see Proverbs 22:6 as a promise; I see it more as a principle. If you give a clear vision and lay down the track, by following these seasonal emphases, focusing on *Heart* and *Obedience* first, then building in solid biblical *Teaching* with a powerful *Vision*, then all of that is a solidly laid out track that they should naturally run on when they are older and moving through life on their own, so it is much harder to depart from it.

Does that mean they won't get off the tracks or go in the ditch? No. But then that is where we as parents continue to apply that *Encouraging* and *Releasing* into this next season to help them get back on track. Here is what is fairly certain. If they have no tracks laid down to run on, they *will* get stuck by all the allures of the world, their flesh, and the devil. When a train has momentum going down a track, it is able to hit obstacles and keep going by the sheer force of the momentum and knock the distractions out of the way.

I remember growing up on our farm in Indiana and it had a train track that ran right through the middle of Dad's farm. Those old trains had on the front of them what was called "Cow Catchers" so if something as big as a cow was in their way, standing or laying on the track, it would push them aside and keep going. One time, Dad was driving the tractor pulling a plow over that track and somehow, he didn't hear that train a coming, coming down the track . . . Oh, got off on Johnny Cash there for a moment. The train actually hit the back of Dad's plow and the wheel to the plow went flying through the air. Needless to say, when that happened, Dad noticed! He plowed all the way home, without the back wheel to hold it up—I remember it well to this day, he was all shook up, Uh huh huh . . . now it's Elvis, I don't know what's going on. The train on the other hand, just kept cruising down the track without missing a beat; it never stopped—the engineer may have never even noticed!

If our kids have a clear track to run on, then our prayer and hope is that when all of these cows and plows, or thugs and drugs cross their path, they won't be drawn in, but will rather be moving along with such clarity and momentum, that they will knock those things right out of the way and keep right on going! Or, as Proverbs 22:6 said, "they won't depart from it." Without a track and without momentum, kids much more likely get stuck and pulled into the ditch of all kinds of stalled situations. "Where there is no prophetic vision, the people cast off restraint . . ." (Prov. 29:18 ESV) So, the corollary is true as well; if you instill prophetic vision in your preteens, showing them their future with carefully laid tracks, when they are teens, those tracks will provide the restraint that keeps them going straight!

Without laying out the *Vision Track* during the preteen years, rather than push them down the track during the teen years or help them get back on the track, you are now trying to lay a track and convince them to accept it and get on it all at the same time—much harder! Let's get into the specific areas of vision in the next chapters.

QUESTIONS FOR DISCUSSION

1. When are children best able to absorb your vision?

2. Proverbs 29:18 states, "Where there is no prophetic vision the people cast off restraint." Why would having no vision be connected to casting off restraint? Discuss how this might apply particularly to the teenage years.

3. Why would the timing of when you instill vision matter? How could giving too much too soon choke them or discourage them?

4. What is the difference in a teenager trying to fulfill their plan or your plan?

5. Giving them vision was compared to laying down a train track. What is the difference in your teens getting into trouble without a track and with a track?

CHAPTER 10

A VISION FOR RELATIONSHIPS

O ne key area of vision is that of dating and relationships. Interestingly, this vision for relationships can also be described in four seasons:

1. Special Friends
2. Dating
3. Engagement
4. Marriage

Carefully laying this vision out to pre-teen children again helps them to absorb it. As discussed in the prior chapter, laying a relational vision track down will help so that when they are teens, they just run on the tracks that are laid. Is there a guarantee they will run on them? No. But if there is no track, there is pretty much a guarantee they won't run on the track that isn't there.

This is an area we would adjust and do differently if we could go back; it's that 20/20 hindsight again! We had observed so many serial relationships in kids starting with their first boyfriend or girlfriend at seven that by the time they were really ready to find a marriage partner, they were all disillusioned and used up. So, we were extra careful and set in motion a vision for "no dating until you are old enough to get married" plan.

We taught our kids that the only real reason for dating and having a girlfriend/boyfriend is to find a spouse, and there is really no good purpose for that until you are conceivably old enough to get married, like around 18. I have friends and nieces that got married at 18, me and now my son got married to our wives at 19, so it's not impossible. We had the "No No No No No YES" plan! The part that we didn't really think through was that it takes some time to learn how to have relationships with the opposite sex and that having a few years of learning in that environment wouldn't be the worst thing.

In hindsight, if we were doing it again, we would adjust that vision for relationships a bit. I still think that kids getting wrapped up in boyfriend/girlfriend relationships too early, in pre-teen and early teens, is a lot of wasted time and energy. However, today we would back that up a couple years and once our kids were demonstrating responsibility at say around 16, this would be a good time to begin opening the door for dating relationships. At that point in life, we would still be guiding them and helping them to work through these things so that by the time they were 18 or 19, they would have experienced a few relationships and learned about communicating feelings and how to relate to the opposite sex in respectful and appropriate ways. Anything worthwhile takes practice, and relationships are no different. Now they would be more ready to enter a serious relationship and move towards marriage.

FOUR SEASONS OF RELATIONSHIPS

As mentioned earlier, we have found it helpful to think about relationship in four different stages as well: Special Friends, Dating, Engagement, and Marriage. Helping your children to begin to own and understand how this progression works will help them when they are ready to pursue this. Any clarity of expectation is all the more helpful in our world filled with gender confusion and relational chaos. If you share with your 11 and 12-year-old's a clear vision for what they can hope for and why, this can create a lot of peace and confidence in your children. Then when they are carrying it out during the Fall Harvest Season, you won't be fighting with all the competing ideas of culture and friends. The fertilizer of this vision for relationships will be embraced as their vision, and you can just encourage and release them into it.

You'll notice back on the Changing Seasons Chart (Appendix B), vision is something that is sprinkled in earlier in the Summer Season, but more intentional as it peaks towards the end as the child is transitioning into the teen years. If there are multiple siblings in a family, all of these vision pieces become part of the family culture so that younger children pick these things up more naturally by watching older siblings live them out and engage in the family discussions around them.

WHEN DO YOU START?

A helpful thing for parents to think about and then to cultivate into your children is when your family will start to have "boyfriend" "girlfriend" relationships. If you don't lay this out, then it will probably start at seven years old and be an on and off challenge from here on out. Now, that's something that each family figures out on their own; we just chose to teach them that having a boyfriend relationship didn't help at a young age.

Also, how you teach that makes a difference. Just because you may choose not to have your kids do the normal early boyfriend thing, you can be careful to not make it a bad thing that everybody else does it—it's just different for our family. Rather than them looking down on others, you can just encourage your kids that in "our family" we do it this way for these reasons.

Most girls will start having little crushes somewhere around seven and boys tend to around nine. We told our little kids even before they had crushes that one day they are going to have a feeling or thought that "so and so is really cute, I think I like them." We wanted them to know about that feeling before it happened—while they still thought that would be "gross" and they were planning to marry Mom or Dad. I told them it was perfectly normal to think little Johnny is cute and feel like she likes him. That feeling is OK and most little girls will have feelings like that. But Mommy just wants you to think of it like, "Johnny is so cute and its ok if I think he is cute and nice, but I'm just not going to think of him as my boyfriend. He is just a really cute boy!" We didn't want our little kids to think it's bad when they have a feeling for the opposite sex, we wanted them to see that as good and normal. It's just not the right time to have a boyfriend or girlfriend yet. That time is coming.

SPECIAL FRIENDS

The first of the four Relationship Seasons is Special Friends. That means you are paying attention and interested in relationships, but there is no exclusive commitment made. Today we would begin this probably when our kids are 15 and learning to drive at 16. It is a low-pressure way to spend some one-on-one time with the opposite sex just getting to know each other. It may be that you spend more time talking individually at a group gathering. You might go out to dinner together. But this is not even a "date" per se, but just spending time as "Special Friends" seeing how you like each other, how you get along, what interests each other has. The beauty of this is that there is no exclusivity in this, and hence no real pressure.

As parents, it's good to encourage your kids what type of things would be important in a marriage partner. First and foremost, common faith and commitment to Christ and His church. Then, mutual interests and goals. And of course, enjoying one another. This season may go on for some time until you recognize that "Wow, there is something special here—I really really like Gertrude!" Then, at some point you are ready for the first level of commitment: Dating.

This should be distinguished from serial dating that the world does, just to party, have free sex and have fun, with no commitment or intentions of marriage. Quite the opposite, from little on up, you want to be teaching your children that the ultimate purpose for special friends, and dating is to find a marriage partner, but that process is a journey.

DATING

I recognize that there are people who don't like the concept of dating. I remember when "Courting" was discussed a lot over dating. I personally don't have an issue with what it's called as long as you are clear that we are Christians so what we do is distinctly different than what the world does. You will most likely date a couple people before the right one appears, so some time in this process is natural. If we were doing it again, I would say if you were teaching an acceptable time to have your first dating relationship it would be 16 or 17; with special friends being 15-16; somewhere in that neighborhood.

The world has no parameters for dating. You are different. So, it will be important to lay these out with your children. Dating is not merely for fun; it is for the purpose of praying for and seeking out a spouse. Now, are you ready for that at 16? Well, you ought to be mature enough to recognize this is the purpose, even though you know that is not for several years down the road. The world says sex is a natural part of dating. That is certainly not the case for God's people. Sexual immorality is usually at the top of lists of sins in the Bible but sadly, in our culture it has become completely normalized. The Bible seems to set sexual sin out on a more serious level when it says, "Flee from sexual immorality. All other sins a person commits are outside the body, but whoever sins sexually, sins against their own body." 1 Cor. 6:18 While sex outside of marriage is sin, it is also important that we teach our kids that sex itself is not bad or dirty, but beautiful in God's design. Because it is so special and beautiful, God has designed it within an exclusive covenant of marriage from the beginning. (Genesis 2:24)

It will be important to help your kids put clear boundaries in place for the dating relationship. If you have a son, it would be important for dads to talk about sexual boundaries that they want to practice as this gets closer to reality. If you have daughters, purchase a shotgun.

When the young man comes over to pick up your daughter, make sure you are cleaning it in the front room when he arrives. OK, that's a joke. But it would be a good idea to have a serious conversation with the guy about his standards and expectations to make sure you are on the same page. Most normal red-blooded young men struggle with a one-track mind.

I heard a story about a young man who was planning to pick a girl up for a first date that evening and he went to Walgreens and purchased three different sized chocolates. The cash register was closed so he had to pay by the pharmacy. The pharmacist noticed such a big variety and out of curiosity asked the young man why he would be buying *three* different chocolates. The young man, a bit flattered and proud of himself said he was going to take a girl out on a date that night, and if she only held his hand, he would give her the smallest chocolate at the end of the night. But if she kissed and hugged, he would give her the bigger one. But if she—and he looked at the pharmacist and raised his eyebrows—then she would get the biggest one. He purchased the chocolates and left.

That night, he went to the girl's house and the father wanted him to stay for dinner before they went out. At the dinner table, the whole family was there, and the young man asked if he could say grace. He prayed and prayed, going on for nearly five minutes. When he was done, the girl looked at him and said, "I didn't know you were so religious." The boy replied, "And I didn't know your dad was a pharmacist!"

One important guideline to instill in your kids for dating in high school is to commit to only spending time in public places: restaurants, shopping malls, public parks, or at parent's homes with others around. If these boundaries are kept, then you take care of a lot of challenges just by defensively guarding your environment. I can't even remember the last time I saw someone having sex at Walmart. The reason we talk about this in the Summer "Vision" Season, is to instill these principles beforehand so that when they start to live them out and begin the journey of dating, they already own them personally.

Another aspect of dating is the level of commitment. For Special Friends, we already discussed that there is no commitment, simply an understanding that you enjoy one another and are exploring further steps together. When you are dating, there is a commitment that you are for each other moving towards marriage. This is not merely for fun, but to honor God and seek him for marriage. Can the dating relationship be broken? Of course.

As parents we are aware that the early high school years of dating will be a great learning time for our children. The first person they choose to date will probably not be their mate for life, but this is a healthy time to grow in relationships. Each time a break-up happens it hurts—but it is much more manageable if the boundaries above have been adhered to. Hurt brings an opportunity to learn healing, forgiveness, and ultimately growth. This is all the more reason for the importance of the *Encouragement* focus coming in the Fall Harvest season as we walk with them while they are living this *Vision* out.

ENGAGEMENT

After some time in a committed dating relationship, then you come to the time for marriage. I still think it is respectful and appropriate for a young man to ask the girl's father for permission to marry his daughter. At some point, there is the proposal and then begins the period of engagement. Now, engagement is a greater commitment, with a clear agreement to get married and a date set to do this.

Much discussion and disagreement exist as to how long an engagement should last. We're probably not a good ones to ask; in the church we grew up in, we didn't practice formal dating. So, I proposed to my wife and once she agreed we had a 2-month engagement and were married. I know, a little short perhaps, but 36 years later it seems like it was OK. At the end of the day, a marriage lasts because two people are committed to the Lord and each other. If it's based on feelings, well, that will probably get you through maybe six months. Then it's commitment with feelings coming and going. An engagement can still be broken without the world ending, but it is certainly more difficult and a greater commitment than breaking up in a dating relationship, but far better than ending a marriage.

The world's way today is to move in together. I would build into your kids strongly during the end of the Summer Season, that as they grow up, they will have friends and many people that just live together and don't get married. But this isn't the way *we* do it *because God values the marriage covenant* and sex is designed for people who have made that marriage covenant. People want the benefits of marriage without the commitment of a marriage. It is good to explain to your daughters that if a man is not willing to make an exclusive commitment in marriage, don't give yourself to him. Explain to your sons the high privilege and responsibility of having his own wife—to love, cherish, and protect! That is exactly why you are taking the time to help them understand the seasons of relationship leading to marriage. That is the purpose of the promise ring and the Man of the Sword—to prepare them to fight the good fight and stay pure until marriage. Blessing follows honoring the Lord in this way.

And while there are many situations where people don't end up saving themselves for their wedding night—and it almost becomes unthinkable by the world's standard—it is still God's best and design. If you can share that vision in your pre-teens laying down that preferred track, then encouraging and releasing them through the seasons of relationships, you have the best opportunity to see your children enjoy that kind of sacred exclusive relationship. When it doesn't happen, you continue to point towards Jesus, towards grace and forgiveness, moving forward in God's plan. Remember the train track—if they get off track, you help and encourage them to get back on. If a couple chooses to move in together without getting married, then they are basically sharing loud and clear that they have no intention of honoring God's plan for sexual purity. So, setting this vision and expectation is a very important boundary in a culture that has largely disregarded the importance of sexual relationships within the marriage covenant alone.

MARRIAGE

The wedding day has arrived! Wow. Now, there is no getting out. The vows are "Til death do us part." And all thought of an "out" should be out. If you have in your back pocket divorce, well, there will certainly be a day when you want to use it—and many do. Hopefully since you've taught your children to have clear boundaries and a pre-thought vision, they can arrive at the wedding day with health and hope for a life-long marriage commitment to build a future family on.

Again, many of these norms used to be built into the fabric of culture more naturally so that intentionality didn't seem as critical. In the 1860's, the divorce rate was roughly 3%. Divorce was very uncommon and only occurred by proving abuse, adultery, or abandonment. By 1900 it had doubled to 6%. By 1940 it was 20%. By 1980 it topped out at a little over 50%. Since then, the rate has steadily been falling. On the surface that seems positive, however, the reason for this is that people now just live together and don't get married. The rate of people living together outside of marriage has increased nearly 100 times (10,000%) from the time I was born until now according to the US Census Bureau!

So, as you can see, just living together has become a normal step before marriage, or marriage is just replaced by permanent cohabitation. Add to that mix now that men marry men, and men that say they are women marry men, and what do you have? Confusion and chaos are a couple words that come to mind. Having clearly defined steps with boundaries and time-frame expectations can really help clear the fog and confusion for your growing children in a culture where the hope of a healthy, enduring marriage has become more and more rare.

Why not introduce yet one more metaphor? We have used the example of landing a big 747 jetliner. You want everything to come together in the proper order and timing. Starting the decent—special friendships. Seeing the runway on the horizon—dating. Putting down the landing gear and fastening seat belts—engagement. Touchdown and clapping—marriage. If these things are done in order, everything works best. If you start the decent too early, flying for hours too low to the ground, a wreck is more likely, and your flight efficiency is lost. If you touch down before the runway, that causes a lot of damage. If you touch down on the runway but don't have the landing gear down, definitely damage.

Hopefully by providing a vision and sequence, everything can come together in the best possible way in your child's own future marriage and family. The trend can change in your family. No matter what your past has been, your family tree can change from this time moving forward. One thing that is important and that Deb and I did was fast and pray for our children's future mates—well, more accurately, often she'd fast, and I'd pray; I figured since we are one, hopefully that works together!

QUESTIONS FOR DISCUSSION

1. What are the four seasons of relationships?

2. What age seems appropriate for beginning these seasons of relationships? Why would or wouldn't it be wise to just let it play out naturally?

3. How and when do you plan to talk to your children about the idea of living with a boyfriend or girlfriend before marriage?

4. How can you teach your pre-teens and early teens that sex is God's design and beautiful and at the same time has boundaries?

5. Why would guarding your environment in a dating relationship be an important strategy?

CHAPTER 11

A VISION FOR WORK

Work vision is more and more important in our Peter-Pan age of perpetual adolescence. In prior generations, when over 80% of American families actually lived on farms and did the things we are talking about in this book—planting, cultivating and harvesting real crops, children naturally learned to work right along with Dad and Mom; they were out helping to milk cows before sunrise and out in the fields pulling weeds at sunset, with a whole lot of fun mixed in.

Today, hard work isn't naturally built in, so we need to be even more intentional, similar to trends in relationships in the prior section. When your children are 10-12, that is the time to be discussing what the next season will look like—you as the parent cultivate a vision for their preferred future when they are wide open to receive it.

FREEDOM & INDEPENDENCE

The vision for work is directly tied to the freedom and independence that your teens desire, which is good and normal during this season. We want them to want independence. We do not want our 23-year-old sitting on our couches day after day not working or providing for themselves.

The challenge is that with freedom comes responsibility, and that isn't as natural to teens, or probably to all of us. This is where the vision comes in—now you are cultivating into their hearts and minds the vision for those activities that will need to be in place to make the freedom they will desire the most successful.

FREEDOM TAKES MONEY

One aspect of having freedom is having money. If you have money, you have more choices, which increases freedom. During this season, it is good to begin having your children take responsibility for chores around the house—they are part of the family and should contribute to keeping the house running. Deb made job charts for the kids. Starting about four years old they can fold wash cloths or put the spoons and forks in the silverware drawer from the dishwasher. By seven and throughout the Summer Season, they should be fully engaged in helping the house run; it's part of being in the family! Job charts help to identify the responsibilities, and with numerous kids at different ages, the charts reflect their differing abilities.

We rarely paid our kids to do the normal chores. We all live here, so it takes all of us to make our household run smoothly, and Mom and Dad need each of your help! It makes the children feel like they are an important part of the success of the household. We taught the concept that it takes each of us to run this household, "You sleep here, you eat here, we do fun things, and you help keep things going." Allowances and those things may have their place, but we just never did that too formally.

MONEY TAKES JOB

It is important to teach them the value of money and where it comes from. So, we looked for opportunities for them to start working in special situations as young as was feasible. Some of our girls actually started baby-sitting and cleaning houses at 12 and 13, getting paid for that. We encouraged our boys to start mowing yards, working in orange groves, having paper delivery routes when they were 13 and 14 as well.

There is a tension in not pushing these things too fast—you don't want to have your 10-year-old working so much that they are burned out and hate work by the time they are 16. That is the time they should really be jumping in with full passion and excitement. Remember, everything in season. So, Summer (7-12) is primarily the time to build the *Vision* of future work that will provide the freedom they desire. If they work too much during this season, it can both crowd out the *Teaching* they need now and they can become exasperated—they are kids and need to have a lot of fun in a disciplined and ordered environment.

Sports can play an important role in fun and discipline, but a balance is needed. We always had as a rule that the kids could be in one sport per semester—so they got the value of playing as a team, winning and losing, and being guided by a coach. That way when they were teens, they still had room for that job we are talking about. Now we never had any star athletes, which was certainly not helped from their father's genes. You may recall the spaghetti . . .

So, around 10 and 11, you begin to tell them how great it is to work and get paid for it. Prior to this, we had a "giving bank" from Larry Burkett that had a church, a bank, and a store all in one with divided compartments. The closest thing I could find now, which is actually pretty cool, is called the "Money Savvy Pig" on Amazon. It is a piggy bank broken into four compartments—Save, Spend, Donate, and Invest. Investing is something we didn't teach about, but would have been helpful. Then they could put something like 10% into the church, 50% into Savings, invest 10% and leave 30% in the spending compartment to take out when they want. This helped them begin getting used to handling the little bits of money they received from chores, birthdays, or odd jobs up to this point.

Good teaching on handling money is not often done, and we certainly were not as intentional as I wish we would have been. Spending some time teaching them the importance of tithing and generosity, of saving, and principles of investing and compound interest are all important concepts to learn to help them with a vision for work and finances. Now, towards the end of the Summer Season, it's time to start thinking about and exploring opportunities for real jobs. Certainly, tied to work is the ability to get around. So, one thing directly connected to both work and freedom is getting a driver's license.

If you have several kids, then these things become family norms that the next kids aspire to as well. Most kids are excited about these things—and if they have concerns, it's good to work through them before they are 18. That is what vision is about, placing into them a preferred future that they embrace as their own before the time it is to be implemented. Then, on their 16th birthday, they are anticipating going in and passing that drivers test so they are ready to drive to that real job they are about to get—all freedom and independence!

A REAL JOB

In connection to this is a vision for getting a "real" job, as I mentioned, it is good to have them do yard work, help clean houses, baby-sit, and those type of things, but really 16 is the age when they can start to get themselves around because they can now drive. Now is the perfect time for them to also get a job at fast food, ice-cream shop, grocery, or other places. Now, during the last half of the Summer Season—approximately 10-12, this is the time when you start building this vision in more consistently.

At this age, they will be beaming and bursting with excitement as they soak up that rain and fertilizer of *Vision*. Wait to start discussing it until they are 16—they probably aren't as excited about the possibility. If they haven't embraced the working vision as their own by now, it is going to be harder to get them interested later, when they will rather sleep or play video games.

During the teen years, when insecurities are running high, it is intimidating to face things like drivers tests and job interviews. When you couple that with the increased stubbornness and/or laziness that can grow during these years, they may not respond well. However, if you put that vision for work in them during the summer, before they are really ready to do it, then they own it, anticipate it, work through the perceived threats ahead of time, and are excited for it when the time comes. It's not new, it's part of *their plan*!

I can remember all of our kids getting their first "real" job when they were 16 and driving. It was always thrilling and scary. A couple of our kids started at McDonald's. One Sonic. One Chick-fil-A. One Little Caesars. Because that vision was embraced earlier, we didn't have to convince them, it was their plan and all we had to do was *Encourage* and *Release* them into it, which is what we will talk about in the next section: the Fall Harvest Season.

QUESTIONS FOR DISCUSSION

1. When should we start teaching the vision for working? Why?

2. Is it OK to have our young children help with household daily chores? What types of things should they do and how young?

3. Why should you or shouldn't you pay your young children an allowance?

4. Did you receive financial education growing up? How could you intentionally train your children about the importance of giving, saving, spending, and investing?

5. Why would it be important to not get our kids working too much too early? What are the things that could be hindered if this happens?

6. What would be specific benefits of having your 16-year-old getting a real job at that time? Discuss them.

CHAPTER 12

A VISION FOR LIFE ON MISSION

A nother very important vision piece for our family was a 3-month mission trip when they were 16 years old. While this certainly may not be for everyone, hopefully this gives you a vision of something to think and pray about to apply or adapt as the Lord directs you. Our church always took youth mission trips every summer, so beginning in middle school, they would go to Tennessee, or Alabama or somewhere for a week and help with construction or various projects, as well as learning to share their faith. This began to give them confidence to be away and preparation for the "big one" when they were 16. At that time, all five of our kids went somewhere challenging in the world, but this vision was planted in them when they were seven to 10 so that they could look forward to "their mission trip."

As the older kids would take their trip, then we would start talking and praying with the next child about where God would have them to go. What this did was truly solidified their own faith at a critical time in life when kids get sidetracked by so many fleshly things. It has a powerful effect of cutting out the nonsense. The parents and the kids both knew that this was a serious time in their life. It would be the first time that the child would be on their own for that length of time, truly preparing them for the time in just a couple years when they would be moving out on their own. They knew they better have Jesus to hold on to.

In all five children, this proved to be a transition time from Mom and Dad's faith to completely their own. They all came home with a much more solid personal relationship with Jesus. It also helped a lot with the *Releasing* part because in this situation, you really do have to let go of control. When your baby is in Africa, you pray and they pray. In a sense, all you can do is pray; you really do give up control. The only choice is worry yourself to death or truly depend on the living God—for both you and your kids!

So, where did we get 3-months? Well, it actually wasn't anything too scientific. One evening we were out with some missionary friends discussing mission trips and they simply said that a 3-month mission trip was the perfect length for someone to have a positive mission experience.

They said the first month is sort of like a fun vacation—so if they are only going a week or a few weeks, it's usually a good fun vacation experience but doesn't give them any real actual sense of living life on mission. The second month often starts to involve disillusionment; the party is over, it's not fun anymore. "I'm really missing home and the comforts of home." All of these are normal feelings and experiences and if a person comes home during that time, they may have an unnecessarily negative feeling of the experience. But by the third month—it's certainly not a tropical vacation anymore and they have worked through some of those lonely feelings and have begun to adapt as things normalize. That is a great time to conclude the trip for the best potential outcome.

For some reason, Deb and I looked at each other and thought that was good enough for us—it simply made a lot of sense coming from someone who had seen it lived out multiple times.

16-YEAR MISSION TRIP

From that time on we decided that we were going to build this vision into our family culture. When our kids were 16, not only would they be getting a driver's license and a job—but they would also be going on a 3-month summer mission trip somewhere in the world. Now, if you aren't experienced with missions or mission trips, you may not be aware that it is not normal for any agency to accept a 16-year-old for that length of time. So, we had to pray and look for options that were outside the box of many organizations and call on friends and acquaintances that we knew for opportunities. God worked out each of our children's 3-month mission trips amazingly well and even customized it to their special needs—which only He truly understood best.

You may be wondering why 16? This is right smack in the middle of that Fall Harvest Season where the key values are *Encouragement* and *Releasing*. It is also right at the time when kids are really maturing and beginning to make friends and decisions that seriously affect their lives and their futures; too often for the negative. So, while it was a little younger than most might have thought prudent, we wanted to give them a true sense that we trusted them and were releasing them. And they knew this was a big deal, so there isn't much time for messing around with drugs or drama. Back to the train-track metaphor, that was a seriously exciting and big track to run on, so it helped to push aside the many ditch attractions that allure kids in during this time of their lives.

You may recall how we were slow in pushing academics on them, starting later than many thought wise, but by really focusing then on *Obedience* and their *Heart* in that season, and adding *Teaching* and *Vision* in the next, later they would develop faster and be ready for more responsibility sooner. Now this was playing out. We trusted them and they knew it. We worked together for a larger vision, praying together about how these doors would open up.

GAINING PERSPECTIVE

One thing that helped to prepare them was that the year prior, I took them through a *Perspectives Class*. This is a one semester 15-week class, taught all over the country. I would find out where the closest one was and me and our son or daughter would go one night a week in anticipation of their big trip coming up the following summer. It was a neat opportunity to meet a lot of good people and go through perspectives on the world Christian movement—studying how missions developed and where things were today.

I remember one time I was in class with our daughter Alecia and an older guy was teaching the class, telling us about going to Wheaton College and that he actually was a roommate of Jim Elliot. You may have heard of the five young missionaries who tried to take the gospel to some cannibals in Ecuador and were killed for their faith; it made world news. And then that teacher, David Howard, told us about when Jim married his sister Elizabeth Elliot. Wow—we were surprised and then he shared first-hand all the events that surrounded that historic day when those missionaries were martyred. He shared how he and his wife were on vacation in Florida when his sister contacted him, and how they went to help. It was a riveting experience. You can learn more about the Perspectives Class at **www.perspectives.org**

MISSION TRIP EXAMPLES

Our oldest daughter, Leah went to Guatemala for 3-months. Our church took a team of people for a 10-day mission trip with Deb and Leah as part of the team. When the team left to go home, Leah stayed on for another three months. She worked with mission teams up in the mountain villages. They would share the gospel going house to house or have church services for the local village people. Sometimes they had a doctor in the group, so that would be a medical trip and they would set up clinics. Some of the local people would walk for two days to get to the clinic and they would give medical help as well as pray for healing. Leah helped with all the preparations to host these teams and then she helped lead them through their week of activities and ministries. She ended up meeting her future husband Joey there, so you could say that trip really had a lasting impact.

Our second daughter Heather went to the Amazon jungle for 3-months. Both Deb and I went to Brazil in the Amazon as teenagers. It is an amazing place—I remember spear fishing for piranhas. They have lily pads six feet across that you can literally lay a child on! Mosquitos the size of chickens . . . OK, getting carried away. We worked with a mission group called PAZ led by the Huber family, inspiring and dedicated people! We contacted them and it worked out for her to travel with a college group going from Oral Roberts University that was going on a 6-week summer mission trip. For the first half of the trip, she went with them, going up and down the Amazon River, helping to build churches, digging trenches, mixing concrete, and evangelizing in the Amazon villages. Then when the student team went home, she spent the second half of the trip living with one of the missionary families, helping to home-school the children, and working on the mission compound.

Our third daughter Alecia went to South Africa, working with a mission called Impact Africa. We had gotten to know the Franzen's family through relationships here in Florida. My accountant was their brother. They regularly housed interns, and so it worked well for Alecia to work with them in their programs to provide schooling to the African children, outreach and evangelism to the Squatter Camps, and help with the Baby Rescue program. That is a program where they have a little box, somewhat like an overnight deposit box at a bank, that mothers who were going to discard their babies in the trash, would place them in this box to be rescued by someone on the other side of the wall, who would see that they were cared for and placed in a loving home.

We had a real challenge at the very beginning of her trip—her plane was delayed here in Orlando because of storms and arrived in the Atlanta Airport (one of the biggest in the world) late. As she got off her plane, she saw her connecting plane leaving the gate! What now? What do you do with a 16-year-old in a major airport that missed her flight? Well, she called us and went up to the ticketing counter, but many people had missed their connecting flight, so she was just one in a sea of people. I tried talking on the phone to an attendant, but nobody seemed to be paying much attention.

Once they realized that she was only 16, everything changed, and they gave her premier attention. The airline actually had a special area just designed for young people traveling that she was able to stay in and the next day she was happily on her flight to Johannesburg, South Africa. It was a growing and stretching experience for both her and us for sure.

Our son Justin also went to Africa, but he split his 3-months up into 6-weeks in Nigeria and then the final half down in South Africa with Impact Africa as well. We had gotten in touch with a pastor's family in Nigeria highly recommended by trusted friends and they were willing and excited to have Justin come live with them.

One day he had the opportunity to drive 12 hours out to a village where they had never seen a white person before. He was asked to preach to the people—so when you are in Africa in a village and asked to preach—even if you've never preached—you preach! Some of the kids would come up and touch him like he was a Martian.

He actually ended up getting very sick with Malaria and we were concerned. But God used that experience powerfully to build his faith and it inspires him to this day. He finished his second half down in South Africa with Impact Africa where Alecia had served. He actually ended up going back there for a 1-year term after he finished high school where he met his future wife, Shelby. We can remember him face-timing us from Africa at a pizza restaurant, secretly showing us this sweet girl across the restaurant that he was trying to win over, and it worked! We love our Shelby.

Our youngest son Micah went to India with YWAM. That trip actually ended up taking closer to 5-months because he went through a Discipleship Training School (DTS) up in Jacksonville for three months before heading to India for two months where he lived in an orphanage helping out with the kids. He also went out doing evangelistic activities in the community and prayed for people's healing. God used that DTS training in Jacksonville in a major way in Micah's life, where his life was literally touched and transformed by God.

On multiple occasions our kids personally experienced demon-possessed people delivered, and healings take place. Again, you can tell them anything you want—but when they have seen God work first-hand, that is something that anchors them in a deep way. The family Micah worked with had a seamstress sew him the local village clothing those men wore—brightly colored long dress type shirts with matching pants. He was asked to preach many times wearing these clothes. And when you are in India and asked to preach wearing a dress type pant outfit—you preach! God used this time and experiences to help Micah grow and process through his faith in an impacting way.

FAITH & CONFIDENCE

In all five of our kids' experiences, we can say that it had a major positive effect on their lives. They experienced first-hand God open doors and, in some cases, really do miracles. I can remember Ron Allen, our pastor in Ft Wayne saying multiple times, "A man with an experience is never at the mercy of a man with an argument." When our kids came home, they had experienced God provide and come through in so many ways that it changed them. Their faith was not ours—it was their own and tested. They watched God provide resources during the fundraising. As they would go to the mailbox and continue to see what God was providing, their faith was encouraged.

Funding is certainly one question that comes up. We found that people are inspired with this vision and love to see kids growing with faith and confidence. So, with each one, we would help them craft a support letter, explaining this special one-time 3-month trip that they had been preparing for, where they were going, and what they would be doing. We gave people an opportunity to pray and give if they desired. And people did—family members and friends would help. Then, when their trip was over, they would send out a thank you as well as a report on how they grew and what they saw God do. Our kid's faith and confidence grew, but it also seemed that others who participated were encouraged as well.

As the kids watched God heal people, work out challenges, and meet them in very personal ways—this anchored their faith. It became their own, not Mom and Dad's. In the same way, we saw them come back much more confident and capable in their own leadership. Once you have navigated the Atlanta Airport, gone up and down the Amazon, or negotiated with an immigration guard in the Dubai International Airport . . . an interview at McDonald's? You got this!

LESSONS LEARNED

Since this time, we have seen many families do the same thing; sometimes adjusting the time frames but generally having experienced similar positive results. There have been some things we have learned that we encourage families to think about if they choose to carry out this part of the vision. We didn't do this on purpose, but it worked out that in all of our kids' experiences, they were living with and working with *a group of young people doing active mission work*—building things, evangelizing in villages, etc. Heather ended up living with a family for six weeks, where basically she was helping around the house with the missionary family. That got a little long, but since she had such a positive engaging experience with the ORU students in the Amazon villages, it balanced out. Justin spent six weeks living with a family in Nigeria, but they traveled a lot and did evangelism, and he was sick part of the time. He spent the last half actively working with other youth at Impact Africa in South Africa.

We have since had other families where their child spent the entire 3-month time just living with a missionary family with not much to do but help with the kids and that hasn't been nearly as inspiring or positive. So, we would encourage trying to make sure they are with a group and engaged in a pretty busy schedule of planned activity for the best experience.

We have certainly found this to be what we consider a real key to helping our kids transition to adulthood with faith and confidence, however, every family has to evaluate your own circumstances and get a clear sense from the Lord that this is His path; believe me, your faith will be tested, and you want to have a strong sense of peace and direction.

Also, this is why this is important to build in during the Summer Vision Season—years before it actually happens. At times we have found parents who are concerned about their 15- or 16-year-old's rebellion they are noticing. They hear about this and think this may be a good thing to fix them, so they now dump the idea on them. Often, if they haven't been planning and preparing their heart, and you as a parent, preparing your heart to let them go, then springing it on too quickly may not be helpful. Perhaps a shorter trip to give them a vision would be more appropriate.

Being engaged in church and a church youth group had afforded our kids many opportunities to take summer weeklong mission trips probably three years prior to when they went on the "big one" at 16. If this idea isn't something that you choose to do, perhaps there is another experience that would incorporate the key elements that impact teens at this critical time: Independence, Risk, Faith-stretching and building . . . all of these elements were what caused them and us to truly trust God and let them go at this transitional time in their lives.

EVERYBODY A MISSIONARY?

You may think that somehow this implies that everybody is supposed to be a missionary. Well, actually you are right! We are all called to live out the Great Commission and by giving your kids a vision for the bigger world, and how they can serve, you are instilling in them a heart for service. Now, this *doesn't* imply that they will all end up in some developing world culture. That is a common misconception of missions and web also assumed that would probably be the case. Our daughter Leah and Joey served in Guatemala for a year after they were married. Our son Justin and his wife Shelby went back to Africa after they were married and served for two years. Ironically, as we thought several of our kids might end up living their lives on a foreign mission field, as of now, each of our kids are engaged in jobs and ministries in the United States in their local churches and communities. Most of our kids and grandkids live close by now—and we're not complaining about that!

We're all called to live a life on mission wherever we are at, and cultures are coming together with needs and opportunities everywhere. A few weeks ago, we had a worship team practice and I had to marvel at who was together—we had Asian, Latino, Black, an old White guy (yours truly), and a 12-year-old drummer and his mom. That is a little picture of heaven right there! Young and old from every culture. Go into all the world, and all the world is increasingly at your doorstep. By giving your kids a vision for mission and service, you are equipping them with faith and confidence to serve and then you can watch how the Lord directs that in their lives—it may mean they serve on the other side of the world, or it may mean they serve in your hometown; or it could mean both!

QUESTIONS FOR DISCUSSION

1. What are some of the benefits from teaching and preparing your children to go on a 3-month mission trip?

2. How could that help you to release them and help them to grow in their own personal faith? What are the biggest concerns or negatives you would see?

3. Why would it be important to prepare for this long in advance, rather than deciding to do it when you are starting to experience trouble with your teens?

4. How could beginning to send your middle-school age children on week-long summer mission trips be beneficial?

5. If a longer mission trip is not something you choose to do during your child's teenage years, what are some other options that you could plan for that might encourage independence, risk, and faith-building for them during this time?

CHAPTER 13

A VISION FOR INDEPENDENCE

All of these vision pieces really have one common goal. As parents, I think all of us would agree that our greatest desire is to see our children grow up to become godly, responsible adults and citizens. Each of these seasons builds upon the next as we seek to do the best we know to cultivate our children into successful adults who will launch out into the world with purpose and strength.

As such, the final part of the *Vision* in the Summer Season—really transitioning into the early teens, is to give your children a vision for their independence. Now that they are becoming teen-agers, they want their independence more and more and aren't afraid to let you know!

The beautiful part is that this doesn't need to be a negative thing or a place for tension, because as parents, you want them to grow into responsible independent adults too. The only challenge is navigating when and how to get there. At this stage of seasonal transition, this is a good time to begin having these conversations—when your child is in the age range around 12-14.

Do you want your child living at home with you when they are 35? Well, the time to begin this discussion isn't when they are 25 and seem to be unable or unwilling to launch; that is difficult and painful. If you've been talking about this season of life since they've been younger as a normal progression, they will embrace the steps to becoming independent. They will *want* to become responsible adults. The teen years can be an encouraging time of life between you as parents and your teen. You will be excited with them about new opportunities and areas of growth for them. The tension throughout the teen years is that kids want freedom, but they don't really want— or aren't ready for the responsibility. Freedom and responsibility go hand in hand; as responsibility increases, so does freedom and that really culminates in your adult child moving out on their own and taking care of himself.

MOVIN' ON OUT

Parents have to discuss this and decide what they want their family plan to be. I recognize that various ethnicities and cultures view families living together differently, so this needs to be customized. Also, there are issues like developmental delays, mental health issues, or failure to launch due to past traumas. All of these things each parent must evaluate for their own circumstances.

For us personally, in our American culture and from our backgrounds, we decided that it was healthy for our kids to realize that when they were adults (18 and beyond), our family plan would be that our children would now move out of the house on their own. I know, I know, if you have a 12- or 13-year-old, this seems like a lifetime away and you probably can't bear to think about your baby leaving.

However, the truth is—it's about five years away! And here is what we've learned. If you talk about these *Vision* expectations now, it's not really threatening or hurtful, but just the distant future plan for them. It's part of them becoming independent and starting to live with the freedom of making all of life's choices. This can actually be inspiring to an early teen. So, for us it was always just understood that once you turn 18 it's time to start figuring out how you are going to live on your own. We taught them that this is normal and healthy.

When the kids are moving off to college, they will be staying at school. If they are going to college locally, then we are open to them still living at home. If they choose to not go to college, then of course they will be working full-time at a job and making a plan to get out on their own. We always told our kids that after 18, our home will always be open for them for transitions, but not for permanent housing without a plan, apart from life-altering circumstances. And life-altering circumstances do happen.

Recently, our son-in-law Saul Rapalo died suddenly of a brain aneurism. We sure miss you son! You left with such a powerful testimony, but way too soon at just 36. Sadly, this leaves our daughter Heather as a 32-year-old widow with two little girls, one and four. Of course, I told her, "You come home here and live as long as you want." For now, she is staying in Miami as she has a wonderful church family and friends, and we go back and forth a lot. It has been extremely difficult and at the time of writing this our family is still in the midst of processing the long-term impact of a devastating loss like this. We don't know what the future holds but we do know that God holds us. We have seen God's love and care through the support of her church, family, and so many friends.

NORMAL VS HURTFUL

If you build this vision of independence in, beginning at the end of summer and into the fall teen years, then by the time they actually get to this point of moving out, it is a normal expectation and not some surprise or hurtful thing. Too often, parents have not discussed this and then they are dealing with a 24-year-old boy who likes the free housing, free food, free utilities, but also may not feel pressure to get up and keep a job. As parents, you are now concerned with how you really bring this up and enforce what inside you feel isn't healthy? It is difficult—but if you would have set those norms 10 years earlier as *their vision*, then it would have just been a normal part of growing up; a positive and exciting challenge and transition.

Most of our kids went off to college; one of our sons got married at 19, like Dad, and worked hard, then moved to Africa to do mission work for a few years with his young family. Also, most of our kids have moved back home for periods of time when they were transitioning—a few months here and there, trying to figure out the next steps. What we have found is that a big part of the success of implementing those Winter Parenting Season values of *Rest* and *Friendship* has to do with your kids being fully functioning adults at that time, taking responsibility for themselves and their families.

FIGHTING THEIR OWN FIGHT

If they are out there fighting the fight to pay the bills and take care of themselves, it is natural for us to come alongside as their greatest ally and friend, being available for advice and encouragement, like friends do! If they are still living at home in their 20's and beyond, there is a tension because they are still under your roof—and in a sense, under your authority because you are still their provider—but yet they are adults and want the freedom and independence that adulthood should afford. When those lines are blurred, their development and your relationship can be hindered.

One of our daughters moved home after college and stayed longer. It went pretty well, but after a period of time, we could tell she didn't love being in her twenties and still at home. She began to seek that independence more by turning her room into a small efficiency, so that she could have a greater sense of freedom. We too, were trying to pray and figure out how she could take the next step; together we looked at houses, and of course those are getting higher and higher priced. Then, one day we were driving through a Mobile Home community, and we noticed a small hand-written *For Sale* sign in the window of an older doublewide. We went and knocked on the door and found out it really was for sale—in rough shape but at a cheap price!

She ended up getting that and hired a contractor that completely rehabbed the inside from top to bottom. She was able to move into a beautifully remodeled 4-bedroom home that was very affordable. For years now she has enjoyed her place, plus a big added bonus is she rents her other three bedrooms to single girls who also need housing. She provides them housing and it gives her a financial boost as well, plus they've enjoyed community and become good friends!

SET THE VISION EARLY

Setting that vision for relationships, work ethic, and independence early creates the best opportunity for everyone to be on the same page when the time comes, all working together for the same goal. Waiting because you want your baby to stay home or you just haven't thought about talking about it, can cause a lot more difficulty later. Every family has to decide what fits into their context; there may be cultural, economic, or developmental reasons in your children that change or affect your plan.

At the very minimum it is good to think and pray this through earlier rather than waiting until Junior is 6'4 and just doesn't want to come out of his room, except for you to feed him. Every situation is different—and each of your kids is different and will navigate a different path. As we just described, prayer and creativity will work through each of their situations as they develop uniquely, and as you face life's unexpected curve balls. A general vision and expectation combined with flexibility and faith will hopefully allow for the smoothest transition possible into adulthood.

During the next Fall Harvest Season, the two values you are focusing on are *Encouraging* and *Releasing*—and everything in this Summer Season sets the stage for that transition. Now, your job as a parent shifts from primary instructor and vision setter to more of a coach—where you encourage them in the vision and instruction that has been cultivated into your children, embraced, and now owned by them. You now very intentionally and strategically release them into that vision which transfers responsibility from you to them steadily over that six-year period. Having some type of formal ceremony to mark this transition helps provide clarity and empowerment for the exciting time of transition that is ahead.

Hopefully you have gathered some tools to use to cultivate *Teaching* and *Vision* into your children during this Summer Season of fast growth. Now, it's time to move on to the most exciting season of all—at least it was to me when I farmed: the Fall Harvest Season. This is a busy time of year, but it is the time when you get to see all of the efforts of the past two seasons come together; you see the fruit of your labors. So, as the air starts to get a little chilly and the leaves start to change, let's turn our attention to the focus of the Fall Harvest Season.

QUESTIONS FOR DISCUSSION

1. How do you feel about your teen moving out and figuring out how to live on their own at 18?

2. Why would it be important to talk about this earlier rather than waiting until your child is now an adult to address this issue?

3. What are some of the challenges of having your adult children still all living with you? What type of conflicts could arise with you providing consistent financial support after they are adults?

4. What are some of the biggest challenges to them being able to move out on their own once they are adults? What are some creative, yet godly solutions? Discuss these.

5. What was your culture regarding this growing up?

SEASONS OF PARENTING

SEASON III

FALL HARVEST
(13-18)

ENCOURAGEMENT & RELEASING

In the fall, now the plant is releasing its seed and the farmer's job is to do everything to encourage that process as efficiently as possible. The time for weeding (discipline) was the last two seasons; fertilizer (vision) is also a product for spring and summer!

Fall is the time of release! During the harvest season of parenting, we as parents want to progressively release our children from our parental control and encourage them to live out all of the vision that they have internalized from your cultivation during the last season, helping them become successful adults.

An interesting parallel happens in farming with crops and in parenting with kids; and this shouldn't be surprising as God's creation is all ordered across so many dimensions. Take the standard corn crop for example. As I have mentioned in prior chapters, in the spring you prepare the seedbed and put that kernel of corn in the ground. The kernel actually has to die, but life springs from that ready to grow and flourish. We compared that to our little children, learning to die to their own will and live under your authority while nurturing a tender heart toward God.

In the summer, that corn stalk is growing and maturing—taking in all the nutrients: rain, fertilizer, sunlight. As that is given to the plant, the plant absorbs it all actually becoming part of the plant itself. This was parallel to your children from about age seven to 12, where they are still completely under your control and you are carefully guiding all of the inputs—watering, fertilizing, keeping the weeds pulled out: *Vision* and *Teaching.* And all of this, for better or worse, becomes who they are. The biblical training and vision you have or have not provided is taken in and becomes part of their person; how they think, how they view authority—God and you—how they view themselves, and how they view the world. All of this is deeply engrained during this season.

But now, in fall a distinct change begins to happen in farming with that crop of corn. And this doesn't happen in a day, it actually happens over the full 3-months of fall. In August the growth has begun to slow. As the season changes, the corn stalk is now big and tall. By September the ear of corn has fully formed on the stalk. Everything is now fully developed but then something happens. The corn begins to shift from taking in nutrients to preparing to give off its own seed. What rain did in summer, it no longer does for the corn in the fall. What fertilizer did in the summer, the corn isn't absorbing any longer in the fall. The damage a big weed did to the development of the corn in the summer, doesn't really affect it in the fall. We never went out and weeded the fields in the fall—what was there, was there and we were focused on harvest. Now, the stalk of corn steadily begins to turn from green to golden brown—the vibrant moisture in the stalk and kernel is now drying and hardening, preparing for that wonderful harvest!

How would this relate to your children? Well, during that Fall Harvest Season in their lives, from about 13-17 something shifts as well. They are no longer taking in the wonderful and insightful nutrients you provide as readily. Now, I'm not talking about eating—they eat like horses. But generally, your 15-year-old isn't asking you as much for your incredible wisdom—even though you definitely still have it to offer, but somehow, they just aren't as open. They appear to have taken in all of the knowledge in the world, because they know everything! This is natural and normal—they are transitioning from childhood to fully adult during this season and steadily, from being under your authority to being on their own as adults.

So here is where we have to shift and recognize this season for what it is, and when we do, it is beautiful as we work in line with God's design. However, here is also when you typically hear about the most problems. Why is that? Because the very fact that they are maturing and "hardening" into their own person means they now have "their own ideas." And when those ideas don't align with ours, that is when we naturally "feel" the need to start hoeing out the weeds, fertilizing in our wonderful values, and watering them with our boundaries. The problem, it's the wrong season for that. The fruit is coming out. The crop, for better or worse, is now coming out into the open. It's harvest time and our job as parents is to steward the harvest in the best possible way we can.

To whatever extent we cooperate with that, the best possible result comes. To whatever extent we fight that, we can hinder the process and actually produce the opposite results that we would like and that is the challenge, and why understanding these seasons is so important. If we just do what we feel like doing, we tend to get it just the opposite. When our kids are young, it doesn't feel like discipline is that important, and we hear all of these conflicting ideas. Today the fad is "Gentle Parenting" which gives the little child endless latitude to express their will and emotions, and they run their parents around like a circus trainer. But sadly, what isn't recognized is that first season is when you are the one God has put in place to bring that child's will and emotions into control. I can almost guarantee, when that child is 17 and his will and emotions are unbridled, then the parent won't be wanting to do *gentle parenting*—they will be doing everything possible to control that wild child. Unfortunately, at this point many of the efforts at weeding and feeding aren't received. *Now* is actually the season *for* "Gentle Parenting." The harder you clamp down with discipline or grounding, the more they push back because they are in the season where independence is natural. That's why it's so helpful to step back and look at the big picture because we tend to get these focuses just backwards.

It's "normal" for parents to dread the teenage years and expect rebellion. If you have carefully cultivated *Teaching* and *Vision* into them in the Summer Season, you shouldn't ever *expect* rebellion. These years that they are coming into are exciting! There is so much in this good vision to accomplish as we encourage and release them into it, what is there to rebel against? We're not introducing anything new; they have a clear plan and we simply want to help them carry it out! We never *expected* any rebellion, and our kids would never have thought we did. We knew it was possible, but they and we both knew if it did happen, it would break our hearts, not fulfill our expectations. That is very different than the typical expectation that they just inevitably rebel; just buckle up and prepare for a few years of weeping and gnashing of teeth! That shouldn't be normal—and doesn't have to be for you.

I want to be clear, in the best of circumstances it doesn't mean there is not tension at times; it's part of the process of us releasing them and them becoming their own adult. We had our head butting and disagreements, but actually, that's quite a bit like life. We'd talk them through and work them out. The goal is to try to work together as a team to help your child navigate through this wonderful transition period for the best harvest possible.

CHAPTER 14

ENCOURAGEMENT

Encouragement is one of the major keys during the Fall Harvest Season of parenting. At harvest, it does absolutely no good for the farmer to go up and down the cornrows cursing the weeds or yelling at the corn. Whatever good crop is there, the farmer is giving everything they have to encourage that good seed to be harvested.

During the teen years, this is a time where independence is sought, and insecurity abounds; looking for every opportunity to put courage in—or "in" courage them will do the most to bring out that good fruit. It's so easy to be negative and harp and threaten—but again, that's the wrong season. You have very little power, so look for the good fruit and encourage them at every turn possible!

Courage is so important. When you encourage someone, you are actually instilling courage into them. Now you may wonder why I would be highlighting the value of encouragement now and not earlier. Isn't it important to encourage your children when they are younger? Yes, but it's different. Your encouragement then is by very direct engagement. Careful, predictable, and thoughtful discipline is actually encouragement to your young children. They may not see it that way, but the result is that they are happier, more confident, and more peaceful—that sounds a lot like courage. Loving discipline gives them courage!

When you are carefully guiding their training and putting vision into them, you are actually giving them confidence and clarity—again, a lot of what courage is. But now things are shifting. Now they are actually beginning to produce things on their own—they are taking responsibility in a whole new way. Mom and Dad aren't as central to their lives. They begin to have more of an interest in being with friends than you. They seem more open to learn from other teachers and adults than from you. On the surface, this can be challenging or make us feel sad that our baby doesn't need us as much. But this is all good and normal. As parents, we need encouragement during this time too!

I want to call your attention back to two charts in earlier chapters. One was the Influence/Power Graph:

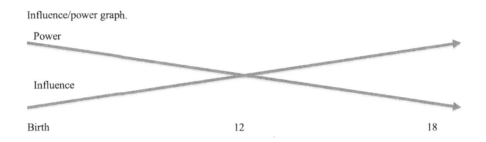

This was the one where the power line on the upper left kept going down steadily to the right. And the Influence line on the lower left steadily rose to the right. This coincides with the Changing Seasons Chart:

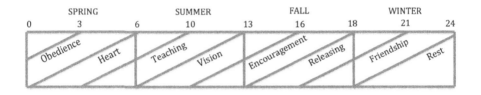

You'll notice that you really begin to ramp up the encouragement right in the middle of the summer season around 10 years old which comes just prior to the time the power and influence lines cross on the chart above. If you will look where the encouragement line starts on the bottom at age 10 and then go straight up to the chart above, you can see the connection. As power is decreasing and influence is increasing, encouragement is the backbone of that influence.

They are now living out the things you have placed in them. You've cast the vision for them to work hard and get a job, get their license, navigate relationships in an ordered and godly way, live on mission in the world and actually go out and do it . . . and now, they are really beginning to! So, as a parent, your role now switches from primary caregiver, provider, authority, teacher—to more of a coach.

If you have taken seriously the major focuses in the prior two season, your influence will be growing in their lives because you have set them up so well for success. You have given them the incredible gift of self-discipline by taking your responsibility as authority in their lives, which now helps them. You've carefully instilled a biblical worldview and a powerful vision to live out, which inspires them. Now you step up as a major encourager in their lives and release them into adulthood.

Keep in mind, this happens gradually over the next six years, so don't panic thinking you are handing your 13-year-old the keys to everything all at once. But the goal is that when they are 18, your greatest joy will be to see them truly taking adult responsibility, walking with the Lord where they *will have* all the keys!

JOSHUA NEEDED ENCOURAGEMENT

Two key examples come to mind in the Bible of the power and timing of encouragement. Joshua and Jesus—Ironically, both the same. Jesus name in Hebrew is Yeshua, or Joshua. If both Jesus and Joshua needed specific encouragement at similar transitional times, the importance of that encouragement may be something to pay special attention to! Joshua had been Moses' right-hand young man for a long time. Moses had been teaching him and casting vision as Joshua had been living in close proximity to him for years, watching and learning. But then a transition came. The Bible says it this way in the first verse of the book that bears Joshua's name:

> After the death of Moses the servant of the Lord, the Lord said to Joshua son of Nun, Moses' aide: "Moses my servant is dead. Now then, you and all these people, get ready to cross

the Jordan River into the land I am about to give to them—to the Israelites.

Moses is dead. Now get ready! There was a specific transition happening. Now Joshua was leading on his own. He wasn't under Moses' watch and authority anymore. But take notice of the over-the-top amount of encouragement that Joshua needed and received to make this transition. Before Moses died, he recognized that Joshua was going to need extra encouragement and so he told him this:

> Then Moses summoned Joshua and said to him in the presence of all Israel, *"Be strong and courageous,* for you must go with this people into the land that the Lord swore to their ancestors to give them, and you must divide it among them as their inheritance. The Lord himself goes before you and will be with you; he will never leave you nor forsake you. *Do not be afraid; do not be discouraged."*
> Deuteronomy 31:7

Notice the powerful combination of *Vision* and *Encouragement*. This is what you are going to do (vision) and you can do it! (encouragement) Look at the power of those words, and this wasn't in private—it was in front of everyone. Be strong! Be courageous! You must go into the land. You must divide it. But listen to me son, the *Lord will be with you.* He will *never leave you.* He will *never forsake you.* Don't give in to fear. Don't let "DIScourage" sap your courage! Why now? Nowhere before is it recorded that Moses encouraged Joshua. You can assume he did, but this is different—a different level. Why? Because Joshua is transitioning from dependent or "aide" as the Bible calls him to being on his own, standing on his own, leading on his own.

This transition is happening now in your children—they are going from dependent to independent. I mean, that's how we claim them on our tax returns, because it's a real thing. We just want it to work, and that takes a whole lot of encouragement. And it wasn't just *Moses* here telling Joshua. Look back at the first chapter of Joshua again. The Lord was speaking personally to Joshua himself at this time:

> *Be strong and courageous, because you will lead these people* to inherit the land I swore to their ancestors to give them. *"Be strong and very courageous.* Be careful to obey all the law my servant Moses gave you; do not turn from it to the right or to the left, that you may be successful wherever you go . . . Have I not commanded you? *Be strong and courageous.* Do not be afraid; *do not be discouraged,* for the Lord your God will be with you wherever you go."
> Joshua 1:6-7, 9

That's a whole lot of "Be strong and courageous!" Three times in three different verses God said "be courageous" and then he flipped it yet for emphasis, "don't be discouraged!" Was Joshua dense? I don't think so—I think he was pretty normal, but during this time of transition, going from one who has been receiving training, getting vision, being mentored to now taking responsibility to live out what has been implanted, he needed triple-encouragement. Both from Moses and from God—three times! But it didn't stop there. Now even *the people* had to encourage him. In the very next section of Joshua 1, Joshua began to carry out the commission, walking it out. He ordered the people what to do and where to go, and then in verse 18 the *people* said,

> Whoever rebels against your word and does not obey it, whatever you may command them, will be put to death. Only *be strong and courageous!"* Joshua 1:18

Now the people told Joshua, "Be strong and courageous!" Joshua needed A LOT of encouragement. Moses encouraged him. God encouraged him. The people encouraged him. Why? Because when you are transitioning into responsibility the natural tendency is to fear. The natural response is to feel insecure.

And let me tell you, this is huge in your teenagers; particularly if you have given them a clear vision and track to run on. It is intimidating to go out and start working for others; it's a lot easier to stay in your room and play video games, where when you fail you just hit "play" again. But, since this has been carefully cultivated into them, they own it and want to carry it out. Now it's your job to come along as Moses and God did and say, "Be strong and courageous son, you can do this! You will get that job. God is with you! You will pass that test. You can do it. Don't let fear stop you—you are ready for this!" And so, parent, let me encourage you—you put the courage into your teen to live out the independence that you have been preparing them for, one step at a time.

I have sat with many kids graduating from high school that are afraid. It's a scary transition from growing up to college life then to adult life on their own. During these times there are a lot of decisions and choices they need to make. That is why the *Encouragement* focus begins already back in the middle of summer and peaks around 16—right in the middle of fall, and the *Releasing* focus that will be explained next, starts right at the beginning of fall—increasing little by little—so that it is completely done by 18. If they are encouraged and released intentionally and gradually throughout that Fall Season, then they are ready, confident and excited to launch out after high school. Intentional focus on encouragement makes a huge difference.

JESUS NEEDED ENCOURAGEMENT

When Jesus launched out into His ministry, His Father gave him the encouragement He needed. Matthew says,

> As soon as Jesus was baptized, he went up out of the water. At that moment heaven was opened, and he saw the Spirit of God descending like a dove and alighting on him, and a voice from heaven said, 'This is my Son, whom I love; with him I am well pleased. Mt. 3:16-17

And again, when Jesus was getting closer to his final trial and passion, during the Transfiguration Matthew says,

> While he was still speaking, a bright cloud covered them, and a voice from the cloud said, 'This is my Son, whom I love; with him I am well pleased. Listen to him! Mt 17:5

Both of these accounts have the Father—the perfect Father I might add—encouraging his Son at moments when he was launching out into challenging times. Again, did God do this to Jesus while he was younger, growing up at home? It is possible, but the strategic importance and timing of this stands out because of the two times it was recorded.

The men of our church are going through a video class taught by Robert Lewis, who wrote *Raising a Modern Day Knight* that I recommended in the last section. He pointed out the three things our kids need to hear and how they were contained in what the Father told Jesus.

What did the Father say?

1) I love you.   "This is my beloved son . . ."
2) I'm proud of you. " . . . in whom I am well pleased . . ."
3) You're doing a good job. " . . . listen to him."

All three of those together add up to one word: Encouragement. And while these things are certainly helpful and important all through your children's lives, there are several reasons why during Joshua and

Jesus' lives the encouragement was recorded when it was. In both instances, they were transitioning in their areas of responsibility and independence. Joshua was no longer going to have Moses walking along side of him, now he was living out the lessons and vision that Moses had instilled all the years prior. And Jesus too was now launching out on his ministry, now He was living out the lessons that both his earthly parents, Joseph and Mary and his Heavenly Father had been preparing Him for all those years.

In the same way, your children are transitioning into adults, and you won't be beside them as much of the time. They are launching out to accomplish the *Vision* that has been cultivated into them and they will be spending more time with friends, at jobs with co-workers and bosses, going to other places for mission service, and this is the time they need your encouragement more than ever: I love you. I'm proud of you. You are doing a good job—keep it up!

Another way you can view encouragement is blessing them. By diligently choosing to focus on their person and character, by focusing on the positives that they are doing, rather than zeroing in on the negatives, you are giving them your blessing. Every time you express your love—it is a blessing. Every time you tell them that you are proud of who they are and what they are doing—it is a blessing. When you point out something they are doing right, that too is a blessing. The more these blessings add up during these years, the more their confidence grows, and they find courage—the courage you have put in them as you "in-courage" them! Additionally, the more you encourage them, the more you are strengthening your influence as your power automatically diminishes in their lives.

The opposite can so easily happen. When the friction happens and the push for independence is grating against you, it is so natural to fixate on the negatives. Always pointing them out, always correcting, always picking, nagging, picking . . . and during this season it will have the opposite effect of encouragement and blessing—it is discouraging. You can diss the courage right out of them. That's why this takes intentionality and focus. I think here of what Paul encouraged in Ephesians 4:29

> Do not let any unwholesome talk come out of your mouths, but only *what is helpful for building others up* according to *their needs, that it may benefit* those who listen.

While this applies to everyone, it really applies when we have teens at home. What will build them up? What will benefit them? What are their needs? Then come along side and bring them that courage.

An excellent book that will encourage you as a parent in this is called *The Blessing* by Gary Smalley. He talks about the importance of making sure your kids leave feeling your blessing. This begins with things like a "man-hood" ceremony, where you speak blessing and destiny over their lives, and continues throughout their teenage years so they launch out feeling like they can conquer the world and the two people that will always be behind them cheering them on are Dad and Mom. I don't know of anything more powerful!

I remember an author once saying he would rather have one boy with too much confidence than 10 boys with none—you'd much rather have to pour a little water on a fire that's too hot, than try to light wet wood! The boys with too much confidence will get knocked down with life's normal ups and downs, but the boys with no confidence entering adulthood will be difficult to light up. I thought about that a lot as we were raising our teens!

WHY NOW?

Encouragement is always helpful, but the reason we specifically highlight it during this Fall Harvest Season is because now your children are transitioning towards independence, and they are now living out the *Vision* and *Teaching* you have been instilling into them during the last season. Now, you want to see them begin to take responsibility and walk out the vision. During these teen years there is a tension; they want to be independent, and they show you that, but at the same time, they are searching for their identity more than ever. Now they want to be with friends more than you. They are getting independence by learning to drive and go where they want. They are getting a job, earning some real money. All of these things are good, and we want that for them, but along with that, they have new opportunities for trouble that freedom brings.

They like to try things that are different. An example was hairstyles. We determined we were never going to make a big deal about hair; hair grows, hair gets cut, hair gets colored and grows out again. I certainly have my preferences and convictions, but we didn't make a big hairy deal out of it. Pick your battles. Many things will pass.

When you as their parent are laser focused on the good fruit—the positive attitudes, words, and actions they are living out, by bringing positive attention to it during this time, it is like fanning the flame of the good that you see—giving them that positive reinforcement to keep doing the right things—the hard things—during this season. There will also be negatives, and at times we must deal with them, but we don't make that their identity or our main focus, we continue to fan into flame the vision and destiny that has been cultivated into them!

OPPOSITE HOW YOU FEEL

Here is the challenge: what you will feel like doing during these times is trying to increase the use of your power. When they are pushing against you, our natural human response is to clamp down.

"You disrespect me that way, I'll show you who's the boss here. You are grounded and I'm taking away your keys until you are 30!" OK, a little extreme, but notice what you are doing in this situation, you are resorting to power. But your power is diminishing each and every year, less and less. And sadly, when you use power during your teenager's years indiscriminately, both your power *and* influence go down. The very effort of trying to bolster your power in their lives at this time actually causes both of those lines to decrease. (Refer back to the Power/Influence Graph in Appendix B) These types of situations play out probably 100's of times during that Fall Season of the teenage years.

However, if you have chosen to properly exert the power in your children's life when you did have it and it was the proper season— Spring, about 0-6, then you have put in them a foundation of discipline and respect. If there is a season for "Soft" or "Gentle Parenting" it is this fall teenage season. But again, often our human nature gets these exactly the opposite. This is where encouragement shines. Encouragement maximizes your influence. When you are intentionally looking for "fruit" in their lives that is positive, then that is what you want to point out and focus on. So back to our earlier example, when your teenager is getting mouthier than you are used to and flexing their independence muscles, rather than centering in on that, look for those things in their lives that they are doing well; that they are producing. Rather than engage in a heated power conflict, pause and point out some good fruit in their lives and center there.

How could this look? Suppose they've gotten their license and they have a job, both good things and big deals that often don't happen. One night Tiny Tim didn't come home when you wanted or agreed on. He may be expecting a conflict but what would happen if you said, "Hey I noticed you got in later than normal last night, was everything OK?" Now, think what would happen if at that moment you paused and said something like, "I just want to point out something. Son, you've been at this job now for two months (or two weeks or two days) and I just want you to know how proud I am of you for that. You are doing a good job. Keep it up. That's what responsibility looks like, and you are doing it. I love you."

Stop for a moment and analyze this; sounds a lot like what the Father told Jesus. I love you. I'm proud of you. You are doing a good job! What happens in Tiny Tim's heart right there? He is encouraged. Your influence has been used in the best way—so he receives a boost and so does your influence. Then at the end of that you say something like, "Now, do me a favor and let me know when you are going to be that late next time." Over and over during these years, look for examples of what you can encourage and point out—the positive crop during this harvest season.

Instead, what naturally likes to happen is that you fixate on the late night, turning that into a big power struggle and you could perhaps win that one. You could impose some consequence, and then you could fight to enforce it, and maybe you'd even win that battle, but it doesn't necessarily mean you would win the war. What you want for them is to maximize the fruit that is coming to bear in their lives, but our human nature is to focus on the weeds in their lives—and they definitely seem to come out during this time as well. The weeds come out along with all the hair and body odor. I'm not saying there is never a time for discipline during this season; we'll address that shortly.

Back to our farming metaphor, during the fall harvest the main thing we focused on was getting the crop that was there, released from the stalk and into the bin. The weeds were a hassle, but they weren't the focus, the crop is the focus—however much or little good crop was there, we were working hard to maximize that. Never was there a time that we went out into the field during the fall and spent time cutting out the weeds. Why? It didn't help the harvest at this point. What helped the harvest was doing what we could to separate the weeds from the crop and gather the crop. How does this apply to your teen? There are weeds and there is good fruit—make it your primary goal to encourage the good fruit, the good crop! That is what will give you and them the most benefit.

EXAMPLES OF ENCOURAGEMENT

This encouragement is particularly effective when your quickly becoming adult children are now out there trying to battle out adult activities in a challenging world. When your kids are now navigating large heavy pieces of metal at high speeds, accidents happen. For most of our kids, at different times, they've gotten into fender-benders, and this is usually a time where fears and the seriousness of life come front and center. This is also the time when you can be there to encourage them on; hopefully nobody is hurt. Cars can be fixed or replaced.

I can remember when our oldest daughter was first driving. One advantage of being "economically challenged" and having old beat-up vehicles is that you couldn't really tell which dents your children added. Leah came into the house petrified, because she had slid on the ice and ran into our minivan with her car causing a dent. I was reading the newspaper at the time (back when we still had newspapers and minivans!) and I remember hardly looking up and saying something like, "Oh don't worry about it honey." Just don't touch my motorcycle! No, but accidents happen when kids are driving, and if you can do the best you can to encourage them through it, it has a powerful effect on their growth. They are pretty shaken. And that real-life lesson can serve as an important growth milestone.

When our son Justin was working his first job at McDonald's when he was 16, he was inspired and challenged and wanted to rise to the top. After he was there for a while, they promoted him to shift manager. One night he called me very upset. Now he encountered a whole new level of challenge as he was trying to manage a group of people—some of them were in their 30's and 40's and not wanting to cooperate. He said something like, "Dad, how am I supposed to get these people to do what they are supposed to?" It's when they are taking responsibility and figuring out life that they turn to you for help and encouragement and that is wonderful. I remember saying something like, "Find the other managers there at McDonald's who have been doing this for a long time and ask them to show you how they do it. They are doing it, so they will know what to do." That was the little encouragement he needed to figure out the next steps.

When they do call you or come to you for advice, particularly during this season, it is very important to be available. They probably won't do it as often as they did, and they are gaining independence, so when they do, don't wait—it's important and the impact of the encouragement is time sensitive. This is a regret that I have. I wish when my kids at college called, I would have almost always answered their call. When your teen calls you with something on their mind, they are ready to talk about it right then. If you are busy with something else, consider that when you call them back, they will be a little cold and not that interested to talk. The urgent moment has passed. The beauty of hindsight.

FAITH ENCOURAGEMENT

During the teen years, as the children are transitioning into their adult minds, this is really when their faith matures and becomes their own or can get distracted by the weeds and the ditch. When your teens are doing hard but inspiring things, they are naturally intimidated and afraid. Here I want to zero in on a specific type of encouragement through all of these different vision fulfillments—Faith encouragement.

It's a beautiful thing for your child to trust in Jesus when they are six at the level of understanding and maturity that they have. It is a whole different thing for you to encourage them to trust in Jesus when they are 16 and driving for the first time on their own, calling because they had a fender-bender, going in for a job interview, calling you because they can't figure out how to motivate McDonalds employees, or leaving on a 3-month mission trip on the other side of the world!

All of these things are stretching and give us as parents an opportunity to pray with them and encourage them that this is what it means in John 15 when Jesus said we are to remain in the vine—or remain in Him all the time. When they are feeling the pressure, you can say something like, "Hey, Let's pray you through this! Let's pray about this situation right now." And then pray with them right there about it—when they see you turn to prayer and rely on Jesus for help, they will most likely do that as well when they are out on their own.

At these moments, this gives them something they can take a hold of because they really feel the need and you are giving them the right lifeline. When they are stretching beyond their comfort zone, they will sooner realize their need and dependency on the Lord. When our 16-year-old son was in Nigeria, he contacted Malaria and got really sick. We are in the states and there is nothing we can do—but pray. He was so sick that he began sending good-bye texts to all of his sisters, brother, mother, and I. Now we really knew he was sick. They took him to a Nigerian hospital—PRAY!

He wasn't recovering and so he decided to just spend his time reading through the Bible and praying that God's living Word would heal him. He spent several days just doing that. As he processed the Word at a whole new level of dependency, the Lord steadily began healing his body and giving his strength back. During these types of experiences, it's more than Mom's faith or Uncle Arthur's bedtime stories—it's real need clinging to a real Savior!

Our other son Micah was in Jacksonville going through a YWAM Discipleship Training School to prepare for his India mission trip. He was out on the beach processing what he had been learning and some guy came up to him and said he needed to borrow his phone. Then he took a gun out and pointed it at him. Needless to say, Micah gave him the phone and the guy ran away. When he told us about it, we were like—PRAY!!

I know this isn't real good advertisement for 3-month mission trips, but the truth is we really don't have control over much. We can feel secure, but we are only secure in the Lord. When your teens are up against challenging situations, this is an ideal time to encourage their faith—fan it into flame. Unpack Philippians 4:6-7 that says we should learn not to be anxious, but instead pray and trust—giving those anxieties to the Lord, with thanksgiving! Then the peace of God will guard your heart and your mind. These can just be nice plaques on a wall until your teen is up against something really hard—whether it's friend challenges, school tests, jobs, or armed robbers—those are primetime opportunities for you to encourage them and cheer them on to transfer their trust to the Lord. There is no greater joy than when your children walk in Truth—and this is the season to watch that mature, it's harvest time!

IT'S NOT TOO LATE TO CHANGE

Try to continually look for ways you can help them take the next steps—building them up, instilling courage instead of fear. Fear and insecurity come naturally, but if you can give them courage while they are trying to be independent, that is the best thing at this time. Look for every opportunity to accentuate the positive. In hindsight now, I see this clearer, and going back, I would have spent more time telling them how proud I was of the good things they were doing, that they were doing a good job and that I loved them. And so, now in our adult kid's life, I'm trying to do more and better.

It's interesting how families are different. In the family I grew up in, verbalizing love wasn't something that was done much. The sense was more like, "We know we love each other, why would you have to say it." I can remember after I became a Christian at 16 years old, I felt like I probably should tell my parents I love them and that was like a monumental task I had to build up to. One day I finally worked up the nerve and I told my dad, "Dad I love you." He got uncomfortable, started shifting a little bit, then he replied, "I . . . like you too." Right away I could tell this wasn't going to go anywhere, which for me was probably a relief. Saying it was just not something we did. Maybe you can relate?

Then when I got married and started hanging around Deb's family, I almost experienced shock and overload. Every time we would get ready to leave a family gathering, the trauma started; everybody would go around to everybody and give them a kiss and hug and tell them they loved them. I was thinking, "My goodness, do you all forget that soon!?" It was like one family gathering had more kisses and "I love yous" than it felt like I'd experienced in my whole life. I was watching as the circle moved around towards me; I was definitely looking for the door.

But over time, I weighed out the two different scenarios and recognized, "You know, I think this is really a better way to go." And I determined that my family would have a different culture and we would try to be more expressive, sharing our love and encouragement. We changed a lot from how I grew up, but even now, as our kids are adults, there has been a lot of conversation still about how we could better have expressed emotion and feelings, so we are still trying to adjust. What is my point here? It's never too late to learn and change from how normal has been, to a new normal. Hopefully, these aha's are happening throughout this book for you!

As I just mentioned, there are many of these areas as we have thought about it and are now writing it down, that I realize we missed or could have done a lot better in. That's part of being a human. We can naturally sit around in regret, wishing we could go back, but the best thing we can do is focus on moving forward, doing the best we can in the season we are in. That will have the most positive results in our lives and our kid's lives.

You can still pull in the key values of the season just prior to some extent but trying to go back two seasons to make up lost time is usually detrimental. So, while you may not love the crop you are seeing in your teenage son, maximize it. Trying to go back to Spring in the Fall and now really instill discipline, usually has the opposite desired effect at this point—rebellion rather than obedience. We will discuss Reality Discipline for teens in chapter 16. Encourage the good fruit that is there. Be thankful for it, and it will increase. If you feel you missed cultivating *Teaching* and *Vision* into his life in the Summer Season, look for those teachable moments and take those opportunities and see what kind of receptivity there is. But the biggest thing you can do to help your teen is to maximize *Encouragement* and also *Releasing*, which is the subject of the next chapter.

QUESTIONS FOR DISCUSSION

1. It was stated that insecurity is highest during the teen years. Do you agree with that and see it, or not? How can your encouragement increase confidence in them? Share an example of when that happened.

2. Of the three things the Father told Jesus: I love you, I'm proud of you, You're doing a good job; which of these is easiest for you to say? Does this come naturally for your family? Can you think of an example where you've done that lately with your teen?

3. Discuss why as parents we need to choose to focus on our teen's positive traits and actions instead of focusing on their negative ones. Why is this extremely important? Share some examples of how you could intentionally do that.

4. Discuss why the teen years would be the time for "Gentle Parenting." Why is that difficult?

5. Why would it be important to always try to pick up and respond when your older teens or college students call? Do you agree or disagree?

6. What are some examples of ways you could build faith encouragement into your teens right now?

7. What should we do with regrets in our parenting?

CHAPTER 15

RELEASING

Now, during the teenage years, you want to release the crop; doing what is necessary in a progressive manner to release your children to accomplish the vision that God made them for. Ironically, that is the exact time that many parents "feel" the need to clamp down and *not* release. Sadly, the prime time for that was two seasons ago and too much of that now only produces rebellion. By believing in them and progressively releasing them, parents are playing into the God-given rhythm and season of their life. By having vision laid down prior for things that are often difficult to accomplish, you have something to release them to—license, education leading to jobs, jobs, proper dating, missions, and moving out on their own—the ultimate release.

Releasing happens gradually over the six years of this season. You might think of it this way; each year from 14 on, you are releasing them roughly 20% more each year until they are 18. At this point the ideal is that they are completely released and now you have pretty much honored and respected them as their own adults, making all of their own decisions. It can be a real challenge to release them, because this is *the very opposite* of the discipline and control you were to maximize in the first and second seasons. The very thing that was optimal for one season, becomes the very thing that is detrimental in another season. Clamp down in one, release in the other; the natural clampers have trouble releasing, and the natural releasers have trouble clamping.

Here is where I had mentioned during the Spring Season that different personality types and wiring are helpful. The dad that had said when his child was in the *Obedience* season "My season comes later" because we had taught this in a seminar, but he missed the point thinking he didn't have to engage then, will probably find this Fall Harvest Season easier. Mom may be more frustrated. We have observed this in ourselves and other parents.

Another family where the mom was the disciplinarian, focused and intent on their careful obedience, education and biblical training when they were younger, got increasingly frustrated during their children's teen and adult years, as they would gravitate to Dad, who was always much more easy-going. When Mom didn't recognize the change in seasons and the need to begin releasing, tension and frustration just kept increasing.

She continued trying to teach them, hovering and trying to insert herself into their circumstances, still taking responsibility for everything in their lives and they were less and less interested in having all of Mom's help. Dad on the other hand was more naturally just a friend who was willing to listen and encourage. What seemed passive and unengaged during the prior seasons, is now what the kids more naturally desire and need . . . fascinating how that works.

On the one hand, this is probably why things can balance out and work out reasonably well for a lot of kids. Many times, parents just live by their natural bent, and so they are doing one or two seasons pretty well because that is just how they are wired, and if there are two parents, they seem to be wired opposite a lot of the time. Dad was the disciplinarian; mom was soft and relational. Or in the example above, Dad seemed easier going and relational and mom took full responsibility for discipline and teaching. Each of these qualities are needed at different times and so they can work themselves out naturally.

SUPER EFFECTIVENESS

Imagine however, if you recognize these things and work hard to adjust your natural bent during the proper seasons of your children's lives and intentionally work together to make sure they are getting what they need in the proper season how much *more* effective that could be? I would say super effective! If mom could see the need for their teen children to have more and more independence and release them into it, rather than stressing all the more and working over-time to discipline and teach their 17-year-old's, it could be powerful.

One dad told me how he sat down with his kids in their early teens, around 13 or 14 when there was some natural friction and had a conversation with them. He told them something like, "What you and I desire is actually the same thing. You want to be free and independent. I want that for you too! The only challenge is how we are going to get there—we both have the same goal, we're on the same team. Over these next four or five years, we are going to be giving you more and more independence and freedom, but all of that comes with responsibility. As you demonstrate at each step responsibility, we are going to give you more freedom. If at one step, you don't demonstrate responsibility, then we won't give you as much freedom." That ended up being helpful, because the teen recognized that the parent wanted the same thing they felt they wanted, but they just had to work together towards the same goal.

Because this family had instilled a clear vision in their children when they were in their pre-teen years, they knew what was expected—how they were to approach work, driving, drinking, dating, schooling; it wasn't something new being imposed on them, they owned it. Now was the time to test how they would execute these things. The more responsability they demonstrated, the more freedom they received. *Encouragement* and *Releasing!*

So, for example, one thing he would tell his younger teens was that driving is a huge responsibility but also a huge freedom. I think this is why so many parents delay driving for their kids—because they are scared, and then that fear handicaps their own children and delays what could be a positive freedom. This dad had cast that vision for driving and the kid was naturally excited about that. Now, as the teen was perhaps 14, Dad had other mile-markers in place before driving that he inspired his teenage sons and daughters to excel in so that they could show they were responsible enough to handle the adult freedom of having and driving a car.

All of a sudden, there are real-world reasons for the child to excel in responsibility that they can really taste— "if I do good in my schooling, I prove responsibility towards driving." Or "If I am responsible in my mowing job, then I will prove I'm ready to drive— which comes with buying gas!" As their parent-coach, you are continually trying to encourage them with those connections. Then, as they continue to demonstrate responsibility, you increasingly release them into the freedom they desire.

Together, this becomes the Responsibility—Freedom Dance. You and your teen working together—more responsibility, more freedom, more freedom, more responsibility. And you do the hokey pokey, and you turn yourself around—that's what it's all about!

ONE SEASON BUILDS ON THE PRIOR

Here you begin to see how the seasons build on each other. By having placed all of these vision pieces into your child during summer, so that during the fall teenage years they are now carrying them out, like working at 14, license on 16th birthday so they can get a real job, taking an extended mission trip, all of these are big deals, on top of the normal big deal that these are school years and you and they want to do well in that. But notice something here—most of the *Vision* pieces we introduced in the last season are not centered around the normal activity of school, they are centered around out of school activities—summers, evenings, weekends; and if you home-school, you probably have more flex hours than that.

Stop and analyze this for a second. As the child enters their teen years, they are thinking about the future in defined ways that start to seem exciting. Thinking is the first step to actually doing something. Every action begins with a thought. As they have spent time thinking and planning for these things, it brings inspiration and passion for their future. Now they know that they are going to do all of these things, and what does that do? It fills the time with meaningful and challenging activities. That cliché about idleness being the devil's workshop isn't famous for nothing. If your teens *don't* have a clear vision for what they are doing that takes almost more time than they have for all the positive productive activities, they will still fill the time with something, which can too easily become negative or unproductive activities.

If they own the vision you have instilled, then primarily what you can do is encourage them and release them into it. Without a vision, as the proverb says, people perish or cast-off restraint. And this really happens during the teenage years; if they don't have clear vision that both keeps them busy and shows them what the next hill to conquer is—job, license, youth group activities, mission trip, etc. then you spend more of your time trying to fight off and direct the normal teenage things that raging hormones and lack of direction produce.

If they know working is expected and normal—then you can encourage them and help them to get neighborhood mowing or baby-sitting jobs. "Here is an opportunity!" And you help them get the job. Then you release them more and more as they are taking that responsibility, cheering and encouraging them for doing what adults do, work! They feel good about that and start to get a taste of freedom and responsibility, and how they go together. As they are carrying these things out, you continually look for areas where they are living out the vision and tell them, "I love you, I'm proud of you, you're doing a good job." All of that together is encouragement—or putting courage in them while you are releasing them!

One of the challenges with technology is that kids spend much of their time in "virtual reality." This is why it is all the more important during this time to release them into real-world jobs and activities. Playing a game where you are conquering an enemy or winning a race gives a kid a *feeling* of accomplishment without the *actual accomplishment*. Encountering obstacles and challenging people while pushing through to a win is very different than just re-hitting the "play" button.

Sadly, we have watched good kids reach their teen years and for some reason their parents think their teen should now all of a sudden handle all the details and take full responsibility to accomplish the above-mentioned things. Getting your permit and driver's license, figuring out car insurance, applying for jobs and filling out applications, signing up for college classes—all of these things involve careful details. We think it is important to work as a team to accomplish these things. We want to release them and set them up for success, but we must be involved in helping them through these tedious details and even do some of them by yourself, recognizing that they will catch on soon and start doing it on their own.

It's the familiar progression: "I do." "I do, you watch." "You do, I watch." "You do." Certainly, the first half of the teen years, you are more on the first two of that sequence, but then you are quickly transitioning to the last two. If you leave them to do these greater responsibilities themselves most of them will struggle to figure it out, not get it accomplished, and feel like a failure resulting in some internal anger. Usually that anger turns towards their parents—lucky us! What we really want is to stay engaged and encouraging, while releasing them appropriately, so that they feel encouraged and like they can conquer the world!

PRACTICAL RELEASING EXAMPLES

Here are some ideas about helping your kids get their first car as an example. There are many ways parents work at this. We told our kids that we were going to give each of them $500 towards their first car; now realize for our kids that was about 10-20 years ago when they started driving. Gas was $1.75 when our first teen started driving—this is depressing. By the time our youngest was driving, we had raised that to $750 or $1,000—inflation. They worked and added to the amount we gave them. They weren't the kids driving around with the fancy new cars, but then again, they were the kids driving around *with cars*, which is a big win. Having that plan and vision allowed us to simply be there to encourage and release them into these big deals! Giving in to your natural tendency to protect and hover will not prove helpful. Most kids want to be independent.

Driving with them and encouraging them on how to take responsibility was scary for both of us—but also exciting and empowering! Helping them find that first car when they were 16 was a major milestone. Then be there to encourage them if, OK when they get a fender-bender or a ticket. These are real-life things that aren't virtual reality. You don't just hit start again. You have to pay the ticket and fix or replace the car—both things our kids did, and we encouraged and cheered them through. No need for degrading comments or yelling when things are an accident.

We found a really nice Mercury Mystique with Heather. She was driving so well until the day the armadillo crossed the road. Why did the armadillo cross the road? To cause a lot of trouble! Some overly caring soul stopped for the armadillo, but Heather failed to stop for the overly caring soul and ended up totaling her car. Again, thankfully everyone was OK—not actually sure about the armadillo—and we worked to figure out the next vehicle. I believe it was an armored Hummer to face the next armored Dillo. No, I can't remember, but these things launch and build the kids by inspiring and challenging them towards responsibility in the real world.

Next, they know they are going to get a job—it's not something you are now dreaming up and trying to get them convinced about, it's part of them. Because the "fertilizer" was put in them early, it is now who they are. All we have to do is encourage and release them to fulfill the vision *they* are already planning. So, we worked together to figure out where to get a job. I often go into McDonald's in the morning and get coffee and do my morning devotions. McDonald's definitely has the best coffee; beyond that, the promotion gets much more challenging.

Nevertheless, I knew the manager and found out the steps they needed to apply. I mean it's not the most complicated thing in the world, but to a 16-year-old, it's intimidating. So, we encouraged our oldest daughter to apply there, and she got hired. Since big sister had worked there, our son also applied there when he got old enough. His brother didn't just want to do what everybody else did so he launched out and went down the road to Sonic and got hired there. All of these things are really big deals—filling out an application, doing an interview, getting to work on time, getting along with bosses and employees. And what was our job—encourage and release, encourage and release.

It is important as parents that we help them find jobs and figure out how to apply. We are setting them up for success, so this is part of both encouraging and releasing. I remember some parents would use these things just to see if their child would take responsibility, so they wouldn't help them with an application, set up their driver permit appointments or help them sign up for college classes. For these firsts, it can be very complicated and intimidating. Coming alongside them and helping them get these things set up is important at this time—it is practical encouragement that leads to releasing.

During these years, you are also encouraging them through the seasons of relationships that they are navigating, which as I mentioned earlier, in hindsight we would have done differently. We were of the mind-set of "why waste your single years on relationships when you can be learning, working, serving the Lord in mission, both in your church and out in the world. You'll have your whole life to be married, you may as well wait until that's a possibility." Overall, it worked OK with our kids, but releasing them to begin navigating those relationships a bit earlier would be wise and healthy.

Then it was time to be preparing for the big 3-month summer mission trip between their sophomore and junior year of high school. That was *really* a big deal that stretched their faith and our faith. They had the vision in place, and this was really a test for us to release them.

All of these things are inspiring and empowering to a kid—you are helping them to produce the fruit they don't even realize exists and haven't experienced, but now they are actually doing it and it is rewarding and inspiring to them. It's certainly not easy—or always fun, but then that's a lot like life. That is why now is the time to release them, allowing them to produce their own fruit by their own real-life work and responsibility; you are stewarding the harvest.

TOO BUSY FOR TROUBLE

Here is something else that doesn't happen as quickly when they are on a full vision-fueled path: rebellion. There just isn't that much time or desire to rebel. What exactly is there to rebel against? You are on their team helping them to fulfill *their* vision. You are releasing them towards independence, responsibility, and freedom—at least two of which they really want! And there simply isn't a lot of time to find trouble. By the time they do all the school activities, navigate sports and extra-curricular activities, work a job, stay involved in youth group activities—that train is rolling down the track with incredible momentum and it's a lot less likely to get stuck in the ditch of gangs, sex, drugs, alcohol, or simply wasting massive amounts of time on internet and games.

Now let's look at the other alternative. By not intentionally cultivating any specific vision into your children during the summer years, now during the fall harvest years, when their mind is changing and their will is hardening, there starts to be that independence and resistance. This is normal for kids during these years. The difference is, if they don't have a clearly defined vision track that they own to run on, then they are getting their cues from their friends, Instagram, TikTok or YouTube. Or they are just doing what teens like to do—sleep a lot more and spend most of their time in front of a screen.

Now, as parents, you get concerned and so you take up playing the harp. You harp on this and harp on that. But this isn't encouraging. The more we see our teen changing, the natural tendency is to try to hold them back from these seemingly unbridled urges and bucking bronco tendencies that they are pulling to experience. "Let me go!" "No my baby, I'm scared you'll get hurt." "Let me go!" "Don't do that or you're grounded!" And back and forth it goes because there is no defined path to release them on—so you and they are making it up on the fly—and at that point, the influences of friends and hormones are more powerful than Dad or Mom's suggestions to maybe try getting a job. This is what leads to the often-tumultuous teen years—it is the tearing and pulling of their desire to be independent and free combined with a parent's fear and protection that now comes out on full display.

It's human nature to want to protect our kids. When our kids were driving, Tim Hawkins—who is the comedian that I mentioned earlier—came out with a video talking about moms and how protective they naturally are. When the kid leaves the house to drive away, what do they always say? "Drive careful!" He said, what do you think the teen thinks you will say: "Drive fast and take chances!" "Cut people off sweet pea!" "Use your road rage if you have to!" And so that became the running joke in our family.

Deb had read *Wild at Heart* by John Eldridge which really helped her to understand the difference between boys and girls. It helped to not expect them to act like sweet little girls. We had three girls first. I (Deb) had to make a mental shift that boys are more rowdy, rough and want their independence. After all, one day God will want them to lead their family. So, God puts that desire into boys early in life. They want to start leading. As a parent, you want to encourage the idea of them being leaders and independent. This book helped recognize how important it is to encourage and release, particularly the boys during these years. Our fears and natural tendency to smother and hover doesn't fit well into this season for boys or girls. That is an excellent book to help you, and particularly moms with sons.

WHAT DO YOU THINK ABOUT THAT?

Another aspect of releasing is to increasingly engage your teens in their opinions and thoughts. One way to look at it is during the Spring and Summer Season, your job as a parent is to tell your kids, "*This* is what you think about that." You are the authority—their job is to respect and learn to live in that authority and learn from you. You are the teacher—your job is to teach them a biblical worldview: who God is, what God says. God has designed it this way and it is good and right. The damage being caused now with letting young people think they choose everything and decide everything—again, all the way to their gender, is incalculable.

But now, more and more during this Fall Harvest Season, there is a switch. Now in their developmental progress, they are transitioning to their adult mind, and they have their own thoughts, their own reasoning more and more. This too is good. Now, rather than tell them what to think as we have before, we want to increasingly ask them, "What do you think about that?" That empowers them.

I'll never forget when I was a teenager, I helped a lot of neighboring farmers bale hay and drive tractors during planting and harvest time. I was helping one of the biggest and best farmers in the community and he had two teenage sons that were working with him. I was just there as a 5th wheel helping out, but I was able to observe how they operated running their farm and making decisions. The dad, his two boys and I were standing on the driveway, and they were trying to decide what to do next. Dad looked at his one son and asked him, "What do you think we should do in this situation?" and while I don't remember the details of the conversation, his son said something to the effect, "I'd be minded to do go plant in this field next." Then he looked at the other son and said, "What do you think we should do here?" He said, "I'd be minded to go over there and work that ground next because it's late and we'll be able to get the whole thing done." Then the dad thought about it and gave his opinion aligning with the second son. He asked the boys if they thought that sounded good, and everybody agreed, and they moved forward with a united, collaborative plan.

Why is it that 40 years later, I remember that conversation in the farm driveway? It was empowering! It empowered me as a teenager just watching. Those boys knew they mattered and had something to contribute. Their dad had the wisdom to include them in the decisions at the right time in their lives, encouraging and releasing them to conquer the world—and in the world of farming, they pretty much have! They walked away with their heads held high and have continued to demonstrate excellence and godliness all these years both in their professions, their faith and their families, passing those qualities now down to their own children and grandchildren.

When they are young, you discipline and train, but then you switch as they mature—valuing the budding fruit that is coming out in their lives.

CLASSICAL EDUCATION MODEL

Now before you go to sleep, hang in there for a couple pages—it's called "Classic" for a reason, it's been around and tested. The Classical Education model recognizes these seasons and takes advantage of them. It is known as the Classical Trivium, and not surprisingly, fits relatively well in these first three seasons of parenting. As the name implies, there are three stages represented in the Trivium: Grammar, Logic, and Rhetoric. They blend from one season to another, but Grammar is from about ages 4-11 (K-4/5). In Seasons of Parenting, this encompasses the last half of Spring and the first half of Summer. Earlier in Spring, you are focusing mainly on Obedience and Heart. But increasingly, a child's brain is like a sponge. As they transition into the Summer Season, that is where *Teaching* and *Vision* take center stage. The child learns and memorizes many facts. Truths of the universe are embedded into their minds through fun, games, and exploration.

The next stage is Logic, and runs from about ages 11-14, or grades 5-8. This is a transition from the Summer Season to the Fall Season of parenting and that shift is happening in your child's thinking. As mentioned before in farming, the corn is transitioning from taking in nutrients that shape it, to preparing to give off its own seed—or bearing its own fruit. In our children, somewhere around age 10 or 11 a shift begins to occur, and that sweet child somewhere begins to reveal a different side. They start wanting to argue about everything. All of a sudden, they know everything. And therein lies the challenge. They start wanting to argue and challenge. And this is intermittent—Dr. Jekyll and Mr. Hyde. And it seems you aren't sure who will show up that day.

What is really happening in this transitional stage between summer and fall is what God's Word calls a child's mind and an adult mind.

> When I was a child, I talked like a child, I thought like a child, I reasoned like a child. When I became a man, I put the ways of childhood behind me." 1 Corinthians 13:11

As a child, you think and reason with a child's mind and that mind is different than an adult mind. There are good aspects—simple trust, not all jaded and cynical; I think those are the aspects Jesus was referring to when he said we need to become like children. But then there are developmental aspects. Children think differently. They reason differently. Their child minds simply aren't developed like their adult mind will be.

As parents, it's good to realize this transition is happening right here—from around ages 11-14, and that is why it can feel so rocky. One day the kid is a child, the next day he thinks he's a professor. And as parents—we are there every day to see who it will be! A great book that helps explain this switching back and forth from acting like a little boy to wanting to be treated like a man is *That's My Teenage Son* by Rick Johnson. This book helped me (Deb) to not take it personal when they were arguing with my opinion and strongly expressing theirs. I knew this was part of my son becoming a man. He was learning and trying to lead and express his thoughts and opinions.

Try to keep in mind that the end goal is that you are raising a man to become a strong healthy leader, and this is God ordained from the beginning of creation. He needs to practice somewhere. Let it be with you. We want to help them attain what God intended for boys to become. Knowing that they switch back and forth from boyish behavior to wanting to act like a man is a normal process that both boys and girls will go through. Expect and plan for it.

Recognizing this should help us with the (sometimes strong) urge to belittle them when they are acting out these behaviors. No degrading comments or jabs allowed. Only encouraging words that will build him up! During this time, you continue to try to inspire them with vision and anchor them in Truth. And this leads to that final stage in the Classical Model.

The third stage is the Rhetoric Stage—from 14-18 or grades 9-12. During this stage is when the child matures, he begins to apply that logic, critical thinking and reasoning to everyday topics and discussions. Their thinking changes and matures and this is the time to really begin to engage them and listen to their opinions. "What do you think about that?" becomes more and more appropriate during this time. Seemingly overnight, your child can better express opinions based on logic. They can debate and make valid arguments—you may have noticed that part. Knowingly or not, that farmer dad I just mentioned was maximizing this stage in the most helpful way by valuing and including his boys' opinions in their farming operation plans. When that happens, confidence and empowerment begin to flourish.

So, in summary of this brief overview of the age-old Classical Model of education, the goal of each stage is (grammar) to absorb, (logic) to understand, and (rhetoric) to apply. This fits hand and glove with increased releasing during this Fall Season: this is the application season. They are now applying what they have absorbed and understood in the prior seasons to the real world. You want to encourage them and release them to do this, and the beautiful thing is, that is what they want too! The better they take responsibility to apply, the more freedom you give them. The more freedom they get, the more empowered they are to take more responsibility and apply.

The goal throughout the teenage years is that this positive cycle continues to increase to where you have completely encouraged and released them into adulthood, to where now you can apply the goals of the Winter Season in parenting: *Rest* and *Friendship.*

CHOICES CHOICES II

One example we shared earlier is regarding choices. We'll recap some of it here. It is so easy to get this backwards and we observe this trend all the time. Parents give their little kids so many choices and control over their little lives. This naturally feels good and empowering. One time Deb was watching a little two-year-old and she was told by the parents that every day they lay out two outfits for her and she is allowed to choose which one she wears. They also let her choose what dishes to eat with, which food to eat; choose choose choose, and it seems wise but it isn't. And it is so easy to get sucked in. Deb and the child were figuring out what to eat for lunch and she didn't want this and didn't want that and wanted this until Deb and I looked at each other and recognized the silliness of it. Finally, Deb just said, "This is what we are having for lunch." And then it was settled. Whew. Now again, with food—the child never has to eat it. But then, it will be there for when they are hungry—or dinner is coming. Or breakfast after that . . .

In the simplest form we would say in the Spring Season: few choices. In the Summer Season: some choices. In the Fall Season: many choices. In the Winter Season: All choices. Following that order puts things in their proper place for the child's development. This can feel stifling if you are around parents where the little 5-year-old runs everything in the household. But the truth is, if you establish for your child that you are the one who makes the choices, they will become more content. That's the way it should be, and intuitively, they know it. You won't have all the arguing and debate—remember, that comes naturally at the end of summer and into fall. By giving that too soon, you are unknowingly sabotaging the natural unfolding of the independence and responsibility you want to come later.

If your young child isn't used to lots of choices, then when you start to give them more choices, they actually appreciate it. It feels empowering to be honored with decisions that they haven't been used to making. If they've been calling all the shots since they were picking their wardrobe at three, no choice will seem good enough at eight; it creates confusion rather than clarity, discontentment rather than peace, and entitlement rather than appreciation. Actually, this works really well in a family with multiple ages of kids. You have to pay attention, but all of it feeds into the vision for their preferred future.

Remember, one of the devil's biggest tricks is to try to get us to do good things at the wrong time. Often it is too soon, so that when the proper time comes, it's already old news and no longer appreciated. Having the wisdom to apply them at the right time is a major key.

Now back to this Fall Season, these teen years regarding choices, now you want to give your teen *many choices*; really any choice that they can make they should be encouraged to make. But here, the opposite feeling emerges. While the mother of the 3-year-old feels good giving her baby choices, quite likely, she will "feel" like taking away freedoms and choices at 16. What we want however, is to be engaging in conversation, asking what they think, respecting and valuing their opinion. They have now grown to where they really do have something to offer. Now is the season for that, It's Harvest Time! Reason together and give them as much say in their decisions as possible. All of this puts courage into them—it is empowering! Increasingly, throughout the teenage years at every opportunity seek their opinion and allow them to make as many decisions as possible.

You want them to think things through and it is exciting to watch them do that!

CURFEW

One example that comes to mind is the issue of curfew. Obviously, during that summer pre-teen season, we controlled when they came home at night but during the teen years, we gave them more and more say about what they were doing and when they were coming home. They knew we trusted them, and they desired to maintain that trust. So, we never had a curfew time that was set. We always talked about it. Depending on what they were doing, we asked when they thought they would be home and if something was different to just let us know. They felt empowered and trusted with choices and responsibility and in general that worked pretty well. If something different came up, they called and when they got home, they would come in the bedroom and let us know they were home—Deb I should say, I was usually sleeping so sound I wouldn't hear anything.

That was part of the Freedom-Responsibility Dance. We would go back and forth working it out as we went. Many of their friends thought that was amazing that we weren't so shook up about when they got home, but we trusted them, and they generally wanted to increase that trust—which led to increased freedom. More trust. More choices. More freedom. Their friends loved being at our house because we did not have too many rules. When our kids were little, we had lots of rules and now as teens, our kids knew the things to do and not do. We simply trusted our kids and therefore, their friends felt the respect and trust—much like I remember the feeling I got as a teenager being around my neighbor farmer as he trusted and respected his sons. Teenagers are drawn to encouragement and releasing!

QUESTIONS FOR DISCUSSION

1. Discuss your different personalities; do you think you are more naturally wired towards releasing or trying to discipline? If you are married, how about your spouse? How can you intentionally maximize this during this season?

2. Discuss the "Responsibility-Freedom Dance." What are some examples that you can think of where you can give your teens freedom when they demonstrate responsibility? What are specific examples where this is challenging right now?

3. Discuss the difference between having a clear vision to release them into versus not having one. Why would releasing be more difficult if a clear vision track had not been laid in the prior Summer Season?

4. Some parents think releasing means the teen should just do everything; how would the need to help them with details of job applications, signing up for driver tests, college courses, etc. be important? Discuss examples of this.

5. We mentioned that if they are busy fulfilling "their" own vision, then there really isn't that much to rebel against. Discuss this concept and why that would or would not be the case.

6. During the teen years, you want to listen to and value their input much more, "What do you think about that?" Why would this be important now compared to when they are younger? Can you share any examples where you've done this or how you may try to do it more?

7. Now is the season to let them make many choices. How have you found that difficult? How have you seen that empower them? Where could you begin to apply this more?

CHAPTER 16

REALITY DISCIPLINE

As we just discussed both increased choices and using our influence, this ties in directly with discipline, particularly during this Fall Season. It may appear that with *Releasing* and *Encouraging* there is no more discipline. That's not the case; you are still the authority, and they are still under your roof, however, now the discipline shifts and how you think of it should begin to tie more directly into real world situations. Hence, the title "Reality Discipline." This is a concept where you learn to let the reality of life do the discipline as you intentionally tie consequences of actions to their real-world consequences. Interestingly, just as we experience the rest of our lives, and they soon will too! This fits well with their mental

SEASONS OF PARENTING

development as they begin to apply logic, critical thinking and reasoning to everyday topics and discussions during the teen years.

I was introduced to this concept when I read Dr. Kevin Leman's book *Making Children Mind without Losing Yours* when it first came out way back in 1984. While he advocates this concept for all ages of children, I believe the teenage years are where it really should take center-stage. I would highly recommend that book, thinking particularly about how you could apply this to the teen years. This is where rather than yelling or applying power to your teens, you learn to allow the reality of the situation to bring the discipline as they prepare for real life. In real life, if you don't go to work, you don't get paid. So, reality discipline for a 14-year-old would be if he chooses not to do the work (whatever that is) earlier in the day, then *he* is choosing to not go out with his friends that evening. It's his choice.

MOW THE YARD

Here is how this could play out. Your 14-year-old son is supposed to mow the yard on Friday and he is also planning to spend time with friends Friday night. He naturally wants to spend time with his friends, but he doesn't naturally like to mow nearly as much. You could go head-to-head with the child, reminding him over and over, perhaps threatening if he wouldn't get out and do the job, and eventually he may do it. Or you can use Reality Discipline, where you tie the job that needs to be done to the fun that is coming later—just like happens in reality. If I consistently won't go to work, I won't be able to go anywhere with friends, because going involves cars, gas, activities and restaurants—all requiring money; money comes by work.

So, on Friday morning you say something like. "Hey, the yard needs mowed today as you know. I know you are planning to go out with friends tonight, but just make sure you have it done before then.

If you don't, then *you* are making the choice to stay home from your friends, because you will be choosing to mow the yard tonight. It doesn't really make any difference to us—it's your choice. Sound good?" Most likely they will agree.

Now the monkey jumped from your shoulders to his. He's choosing. You've explained the choice, he gets to make it. That's what independence looks like, choices. Now what happens if 5-o-clock comes around when he needs to get ready to go and he hasn't mowed the yard? Then you remind him of the choice *he made to mow the yard in the evening.* He will not like that—but you knew it, he knew it, and he made it. In the morning it was fine and reasonable.

As a parent, now it's your job to follow through on his choice which can be the hard part. Next Friday, he will be more aware of the reality of the situation. The good part of this is now rather than just being upset at you, he better realizes that he made the decision about what he wanted, mow earlier and enjoy friends, or wait and mow later. He may not like it and can still blame you—but the truth is, he understood it and chose what he did. The same can be utilized for all kinds of household responsibilities—dishes, laundry, trash, etc.

ENCOURAGEMENT WITH DISCIPLINE

As they get older this gets more and more tangible. You want to continue to encourage the responsible things and tie the irresponsible to their natural consequences. This "Reality Discipline" follows the *Encouragement* focus that comes during the Fall Harvest Season. Back on the Changing Seasons chart in Appendix B, you'll notice the *Encouragement* focus starts to be incorporated in the middle of summer, around age 10 and peaks in the middle of fall around 16. That is also when you begin to incorporate Reality Discipline as you begin the transition between the more direct discipline of spanking that was done earlier. Right around 10 or 11, their minds are beginning to change. We just talked through the Classical Model of education, and that is when the "Logic" stage happens—where the child starts to want to argue and challenge more. During that time is when you begin to maximize that change in thinking by beginning to incorporate reality to their discipline, tied directly to their choices whether to do the right thing or not.

Reality Discipline coincides with Encouragement—when you think of encouraging, it all sounds positive, and by enlarge, it is best to focus on the good fruit much more than the negative. However, there is a time to deal with their negative actions—and that is where Reality Discipline comes in to "encourage" them to do the right thing increasingly towards the end of Summer and throughout the Fall.

CLEAN YOUR ROOM

I can remember when our boys were in their early teens, their rooms were just getting out of hand. We had never made a huge deal about super clean rooms—another thing in hindsight, we would probably do better, but now as 14-year-olds, the floor was piled 3' high, or it seemed like that. We had various conflicts and threats and spats. Then in a flash of insight, I decided to apply these Reality Discipline tactics. We had them get their room cleaned up the way we wanted it, and then I put a chart on the wall with a picture of the clean room. I would come up at night before bed and take a look and charged them for each item that was out of place—I think it was a couple dollars per item and I wrote the balance in the box for that day. I was still the authority. They are living in my house, so I had the prerogative to charge "rent" if things weren't the way I wanted, but I wasn't upset or mad about it.

At this point they were really valuing money and had numerous jobs they were doing, trying to make money to get the things they wanted. At the end of the week, they had to pay their cleaning fees. I told them it didn't make me too much difference which they chose, because that was just more date money for Mom and me, which I liked. It was their choice whether they wanted a clean room or wanted to pay us to clean it. Over the next few weeks, that problem cleared up quite well, and then they actually started to appreciate the value of order a bit more as well.

SNOOZE YOU LOSE

When your kids are younger, you are the one that helps them start their days; wake them up at the proper time to get to school on time, get their clothes on, eat breakfast, etc. I remember when one of our boys was driving and had a morning job at a restaurant. Deb would still wake them up if she saw they were oversleeping—you don't want them to be late for work you know. But at some point, you aren't helping them by taking that responsibility for them, so she decided to implement Reality Discipline; it was time to let reality take over. She had a very clear conversation with him telling him he was now old enough to take responsibility to get himself up and ready for work, and that she wasn't going to come in and wake him if he overslept. He thought that seemed very reasonable and readily agreed.

But then, the next morning came. She heard the snooze alarm going—BEEP, BEEP, BEEP, BEEP . . . But no activity, not a creature was stirring! This went on for a long time, and before that conversation, she would be up reminding him that he was going to be late for work, but not this time. Then all of a sudden it was like a bomb went off—things were banging around, loud steps, doors slamming, as he finally woke up and realized he was late. He tore down the steps and left the house. He let her know in no uncertain terms he was not happy. He was late for work. That's reality. It was all mom could do to let it happen. Later, on his drive to work he called and apologized for getting so upset, because he knew it was really on him, and he had even happily agreed to it. Interestingly, that was one of the last times that happened.

That's reality. If I don't pay my electric bill, they shut it off. If I don't, they do. It's my choice. If I don't pay my rent, I get evicted. If I don't pay my mortgage, the bank takes the house. If I don't pay for gas, my car won't run. If I don't get out of bed, I'll be late for work. The more we can tie the reality of situations to their natural consequences, it gives them the ability to choose which they want, learning to see and make the connection. Rather than just your word to try to stop them—it's them choosing which they prefer. Do I want to do the work now, or do I want to do it later? If I do it now, I can do what I like later. If I clean my room now, I don't have to pay. If I want to pay, I can forget my room. Do I want to listen to my alarm, or ignore it? Everything has consequences. That's reality.

QUESTIONS FOR DISCUSSION

1. What is Reality Discipline in your words? Can you describe it and discuss some examples?

2. Why would this be effective?

3. Why would the concept of Reality Discipline be more important during the teen years than the early years?

4. It takes planning and forethought to implement Reality Discipline. Why is it important to get your teens agreement ahead of time? Why would it be difficult to follow through when they make the choice not to do the agreed upon item and pay the reality consequences?

5. We discussed some examples of allowing reality to do the discipline; can you think of any other examples of challenging situations and how you could come up with a plan to let reality cause the discipline?

SEASONS OF PARENTING

CHAPTER 17

TIME TO HARVEST

This is the harvest time! Now is truly the time to celebrate every victory of independence and responsibility that comes along. Parents are still actively involved, just as no crop harvests itself—the farmer has a big role to play. At every turn, you are looking for ways to encourage the responsible things, guiding that crop into the harvester, separating the weeds from the good seed, but focusing on the good seed, not on the weeds. Harvest is really the culmination of everything that has been done before and is truly the time for celebration and Thanksgiving!

As parents, increasingly releasing them as they grow from 14 to 18 can be difficult, but it's important to continually recognize that this is good, and you are working with God's design and the natural rhythm of their growing up seasons. Now you have the pleasure of reaping the reward of all of those years of intentional seasonal focus that you have invested before. The teen years are now truly the culmination of seeing all of these things converge: *Obedience* and *Heart* that was instilled in spring, then adding to that *Teaching* and *Vision* in the summer years—now it's Harvest Time, where the prior seasons investment comes out and you *Encourage* and *Release* them into a life of fruitfulness!

FAVORITE TIME OF YEAR

For me when I used to farm, fall harvest was my absolute favorite time of the year. We got to see the results of all of those months of effort and faith; now it all came together, and we got to experience the fruit of all that labor. Don't confuse that with easy or relaxing—it was actually one of the busiest seasons. And it wasn't all neat and tidy either—it was hectic. I can remember times when our combine (harvesting machine) got plugged up because of the weeds, and I was out on the ground, wrenching around with heavy metal bars, trying to manually unplug the throat of the harvester.

One time, when I was a kid, I remember my dad running home from the field yelling, "The combine's on fire!!" All that corn dust had plugged up the air-filters and caused the engine to heat up until it actually spontaneously combusted.

But, for all the work and challenge, it was the time of transition leading to reward—where the crop went from out in the fields to in the bins for future seed or food! For you and your kids—this is the season of harvest, a time of transition leading to reward. The more you can recognize that and spend your focus encouraging the good fruit and releasing them from your control and responsibility, to where *they* take responsibility, the goal of fall harvest will be realized.

You are preparing your teen to be on their own. They will make mistakes and go down wrong paths. As their parent, treat them with love and respect when they come to you with regret. Part of Reality Discipline is sitting back and watching them make bad decisions and then they have to live through and pick up the mess of those decisions. This too is a time for us to encourage them. We are still their ally and cheering them on, but this is not the season to take control and fix all their problems. They are becoming adults and learning responsibility.

Easy or neat would not be words to describe this time in parenting. Sometimes the weeds plug up the system and you are working to get things unplugged and moving again. Sometimes the friction and tension with your teens causes spontaneous combustion and meltdowns. All of that happens—but the big picture is you are stewarding the harvest, releasing your kids into adulthood and a life of their own productivity, where, before you can imagine, they will have their own babies and be repeating this entire process! What a joy to learn to work in cooperation with God's design and rhythms.

QUESTIONS FOR DISCUSSION

1. Share some examples of the good fruit you have been able to celebrate with your teens as they are maturing and taking responsibility?

2. We mentioned that during harvest, sometimes the weeds plug up the machine. What are examples with your teens where you get bogged down and find it difficult to move forward? Discuss some possible ways forward.

3. We also mentioned spontaneous combustion. What are some examples where you feel like things have heated up to the point of melt-down? What are the issues? What combination of encouragement, releasing, and reality discipline might help to cool down the situation and move forward? Talk it through.

4. Sometimes our teens go down wrong paths, make bad decisions and experience consequences. That's reality. Share some examples of that and how you did or could encourage them without taking responsibility for their choices?

SEASON IV

WINTER REWARD
(18 AND BEYOND)

RESTING AND
FRIENDSHIP

Winter is a wonderful season of reward: Rest and Friendship. The hard work and push of the harvest season is over. The job is largely done. Now is truly the time to enjoy the reward and fruit of all your labors. This was the time we would take all the grain and sell it and enjoy the reward and profits of all the hard work. Winter was less stressful and more relaxed. Sure, you had projects and preparation for spring, but there was more time for family, relationships, and holidays. Up north, outside the ground was frozen and often snow-covered and there wasn't nearly as much direct engagement in producing the crops. The pressure of spring planting and fall harvest was off.

During the winter season of parenting, your children truly are adults, and this is a whole new world for parenting—and for us, one we never even thought about how challenging it can be to try to navigate properly. The three prior seasons last around six years, with blending between seasons. The winter season was different—it starts around 18 and continues indefinitely. But we have observed something very interesting—just as each of the prior seasons lasted around six years, some amazing transformations happen during the first six years or so of your child's adulthood. You have worked to encourage the fruit of their lives and release them into the world to battle life out. Now, they are truly making their own decisions, often bouncing around to different ideas and activities, truly settling into who they are and what they believe.

These years can be difficult, because you want them to be wise, love God, and make good decisions, but now you truly have no power over them . . . and you can really wonder if you have any influence at times as well. During these years, they often have a lot of optimism, which is a good thing. They still think that they know a lot more than they really do, and up until now, you as the parent have been a constant present force in their lives helping to guide and launch them through those harvest years of fall.

THE REAL WORLD

But now an interesting transition happens. They are interacting with the world—all of the philosophies, all of the influences, all of the different types of people—largely on their own without your constant presence and *wise* counsel or cautions. As teens, it was easy to blame you or get mad at you for stuff—you were there as a natural target, still their authority figure. But now, as adults, you aren't there as much and they have to deal with their own decisions, their own weaknesses, and their own consequences.

During these first six years of the Winter Season, there have been many discussions with our kids of things we didn't do right as parents—which is one reason we have waited until now to write this book. That's certainly not always fun or easy to hear, but it's important to listen, bite your tongue, try to learn, apologize at times, and seek to continue moving forward. We believe family is forever, therefore there is always forgiveness and love to be shown. Talking things out and sometimes agreeing to disagree is part of living life with adult kids. A lot of discovery is taking place during these early years of adulthood for them. Things that may not have seemed ideal to them growing up can cause them to lean another direction; if they have been raised very conservative, liberal can feel well, liberating! But give it some time. Watch and pray.

Everywhere they go, they are dealing with real people; sometimes these new friends or acquaintances seem to have such a liberating message, cutting loose the bonds of those suffocating "Puritanical roots" they may think. But just wait—these are all just people, and often they are hurting people who end up hurting people. It just takes a little while to recognize that, as your kids then eventually become the recipient of the hurt. Over those first six years during this Winter Season, they will have dealt with friends, professors, bosses, friends, and more bosses and have been knocked around quite significantly by life . . . and now interestingly, you are not the *cause* or the *solution* or even *part* of the problem.

YOU'RE SMARTER THAN THEY THOUGHT

During those years as they are trying to figure out how to make life work in the real world, you will seem much smarter to them when they are 25 than when they were 14 or even 18. The quote from Mark Twain is true, "When I was a boy of 14, my father was so ignorant I could hardly stand to have the old man around. But when I got to be 21, I was astonished at how much the old man had learned in seven years." The things they may have thought you were outdated or ignorant on, now start to seem a bit wiser to them and this seems to come full circle around 25, which ironically is when biologists tell us our body has reached its maximum prime development—it's all downhill from there!

Hold on and continue to trust, seeking to apply these two focuses of the Winter Parenting season, *Friendship* and *Rest*, that we'll lay out here. A shift takes place somewhere around 23-27 now that they have seen and experienced quite a lot as adults, and they really do recognize that they don't know as much as they thought they did at 18. Their optimism has been challenged—not by old timey-Dad or Mom, but actually by all those other enlightened people and circumstances.

Just this weekend, we had more confirmation regarding this. We have tried very hard to rest from control and responsibility, as we'll discuss next, sometimes with more success than others. We have left them be adults and respected their boundaries the best we knew how. And just this weekend, all of the kids and grandkids were home and the siblings were talking and one of our kids said something like this to Deb, "I know Mom you try really hard not to give advice or share too much of your opinion, but now that we're all older, I think we have figured out more who we are as adults, and I think we would like for you to share your opinions and advice more freely." Yes!! Let's all join together in the Hallelujah Chorus!

CHAPTER 18

RESTING

In farming, once the harvest was in, winter steadily came as the trees were bare, the temperatures froze, and snow began to blanket the fields that just a few months before were receiving all kinds of attention planting, cultivating and harvesting. Now, they lay quiet and frozen. As farmers, winter was a wonderful time of rest and reward; in some ways, the rest was forced as there simply wasn't as much activity to do. We would spend time preparing for the next spring; working on equipment, cleaning up things that were neglected during the busy seasons prior. But also—it was simply a time to refresh and rest. Without the pressure to get as much accomplished a natural time of replenishing occurred. Winter was when Dad and

Mom would often take time to drive down to Florida for a vacation. The pace seemed slower as the rhythms of work and rest naturally played out in life.

You may wonder how this would equate with parenting. Now that your child is an adult, it is important that you take a rest from most of the activities you were focused on during the prior seasons. If, when I was farming, in my need to feel productive and keep busy, I would have taken the tractor out in the snow-covered field and pulled a corn-planter around, depositing seed, it would have produced nothing helpful. It would have attracted attention, but not the kind you'd really want. Why? It was the right thing . . . at the wrong time.

Occasionally, we would still see a cornfield standing in January when there was snow on the ground. And you may even see the farmer out there with the combine harvesting it. Remember, you can still introduce the focuses of the season directly prior, but with diminished effectiveness. That farmer was getting some corn, but nobody was waiting at the end of the field asking him for tips on effective farming; you actually felt a little sorry for the guy because something wasn't going too super. Much of the corn had fallen down because the prime season for harvest had passed and his crop was greatly diminished.

RESTING FROM RESPONSIBILITY

Winter in parenting is the time to rest from taking responsibility for your adult children. This is truly a challenge, but when your children are adults, now you are equals and you are no longer responsible for them. Now you sure can still "feel" responsible for them, but they are now adults. During the fall teenage season, you were increasingly releasing them—taking less and less responsibility and giving them more, preparing for this time. But now, you truly are not responsible. That is the difference. *Releasing* and *Resting* can seem the same, but they are not. All through the six years of *Releasing* during the Fall Harvest Season, you still had control, but you were increasingly letting it go. With *Resting*, you are done. You need to completely let go of responsibility and control. And I will tell you, this is a big adjustment for parents to make and kids to take.

On the face of it, this could appear like you don't care or aren't helpful. But actually, it is just the opposite. You care so much about them, that you are truly giving them what is theirs to have—adult responsibility, and they will respect you for it. Rather than still viewing them as children, taking upon yourself their affairs, you respect them enough to let them have what is rightfully theirs. If you have attentively and increasingly released responsibility over the prior six years, then this should be a natural final step of total releasing.

TREAT THEM LIKE ADULTS

So, when they are facing a problem or doing something that you don't think is the wisest, you don't immediately jump in there as a savior—they have Him, and we're not it. Now, does this mean you aren't willing to help? Well, it depends in what ways. You see, sometimes kids enjoy having you taking the responsibility that should be theirs—it's easier, but it's not empowering. It's not building their adult dignity and it can keep them stifled and dependent. Also, sometimes parents enjoy taking the responsibility—and I think this is the bigger problem. I like being important and needed. It feels like we have value when we step in and rescue and fix and do all the things that parents of *children* do. But here is the news flash that has crept up on us quicker than we can believe: They are no longer children. They are adults and now we need to treat them as adults.

How do you treat your adult siblings for instance? Do you call them and make sure they have paid their electric bill? Do you ask them when you see them if they have changed the oil in their car lately? I doubt it. When you intentionally rest completely from taking responsibility for them, while it may feel a little challenging for both of you, they will respect you for it and they will naturally *want to be with you more.* You are valuing them as a peer and an adult, something they really desire.

Part of resting from responsibility is intentionally choosing not to give all of that incredible advice that we have stored up. I know, it is such a pity not to use it all! But, as adults, and particularly in this first 6-years of the Winter Season of parenting, keep most of it to yourself. Start a blog or something. Or—write a book, that's how I'm coping with getting my pent-up advice out! When it comes to your adult kids, less is more. Here is the truth. Are you ready? *They really do know nearly everything you think on everything.* They do! We have told them many many times throughout their lifetime.

But here is something that is really rewarding during this Winter Season. If you respect them as adults and rest from taking their responsibility, and as you develop the friendship we will talk about in the next chapter, they will sometimes ask you for your advice. We try really hard never to insert our advice unless they ask—then our challenge is when they do finally ask, not to back up the truck and dump every bit of it that has been wanting to burst out for the prior months. Seems like we've experienced this, I know.

A book that is fitting and highly recommended during this Winter Rest and Friendship Season is titled, *Doing Life with your Adult Children: Keep Your Mouth Shut and the Welcome Mat Out* by Jim Burns. The title pretty much says it all and we have been helped by this and recommended it to so many parents as they are going through that challenging season of now having adult children. We never even thought of that season as being tough, but it is, particularly the "keep your mouth shut" part!

RESTING FROM CONTROL

A close cousin to responsibility is control—but deserving separate attention because it's such a tendency. In the spring, when your child is 0-6 you should have total control, yet it seems so many parents fail to recognize or take this responsibility. Then, during the fall you are releasing control and now in winter, you should have *no* control. We shouldn't try to hold over them our expectations, because that is control. They know our desires, but we cannot control them. Sadly, sometimes we parents are the last to find out. This is the season to truly give it to God and stop trying to be in control of anything in their lives. The more control you do try to exert in their lives during this season, you will notice that they deal with that by simply not being around as much! Now *they* can control how much they are around you—if you continue trying to mother and smother them as adults, they will simply get away from your ability to do that.

NOW THAT I'M 18

As part of the vision we instilled, we had told our kids that when they are 18, they are adults and we will no longer control them. I remember when our son turned 18. We had taught and expected that all of our kids would go to college . . . another thing that may not have been right, but that's the way it was. About five minutes after our son turned 18, I went out to lunch with him and he said something like this, "Dad, now that I'm 18, is it right for you to have an expectation that I go to college?" Long pause . . . he had me. If I'm not controlling them now, then how can I have these expectations? So, I said right away, "You are right. I shouldn't have an expectation—I can desire that you would go to college, but I shouldn't expect you to. It's up to you now what you decide to do." I recognized that was true and I released it and then he chose a different path of working hard, doing missions, and starting a family young—and he's figuring it out quite well.

Often, teens don't have the ability to get out from the control, but if it is *not* released appropriately, they will often get out from under that just as soon as possible. If they become adults and we still haven't recognized their need for release, they will often see to it that it happens. One of the most common things we have experienced is hovering helicopter parents that just feel such a worry and need to suffocate their adult children, and the older kids simply don't want that. That's why this winter season is challenging—it is challenging for us as parents to let go.

A NEW EXPANDED FOCUS

One thing we have noticed that helps parent's transition during this Winter Reward Season of parenting is to be actively engaged in meaningful work. Now is a time to explore hobbies or new expanded ministry opportunities you always desired to do but did not have time for. Depending on when you started your family, this season can start anywhere from 40 and still be happening up around 60. In order to fill the void that their physical absence, and your absence of control in their lives brings, this may be a good time to engage in a new expanded career or ministry role in your own life. It serves two purposes; one is that you are inspired with something new and meaningful to pursue at a time when you are needed less by your kids, and two is that they are inspired by seeing you engaged and fulfilled, without needing to find your identity in over-involvement and control in their lives.

Particularly moms, if they have been fully engaged in parenting, as the Fall Season starts and the Winter Season comes, this may be a great time to look for a new opportunity in your own life and career. We've known moms who after the kids grew up went back to school, went back into their professions, or jumped in and fully engaged in the family business. Our adult kids are inspired when they observe us still growing, learning, trying new things and engaged in meaningful work and ministry. The parent that has been so wrapped up in their child's development—often doing an outstanding job of *Heart*, *Obedience*, *Teaching*, and *Vision* in the first two seasons, if they don't transition themselves during the Fall and Winter Seasons of parenting, can sometimes later cripple and suffocate their kids.

A dad or mom who flounders with loss of identity after their baby has gone off to college resulting in the parents need to constantly check in, advise, help, check-in, advise, help . . . will hinder the child's development and cause them to struggle with respecting and desiring to be close to their parents. The very thing the parent would desire, having influence and friendship with their child, is hindered because they themselves haven't transitioned.

When you are putting *Vision* into your children during the Summer Season, it is wise to also look at *a renewed vision for your own life* and how you may adjust and change, asking the Lord what He may have for you as your kids are needed much less by you. It is a great combination to have vision in place that your kids have pursued during their teen years and have a vision for yourself for what you will do to fill that void after the teenage years. Both of these will work together towards maximum reward during the Winter Season in parenting.

RESTING FROM PROVISION

Provision also has a bearing on control. During the Fall Season, the teens are wanting freedom and our goal as parents is to increasingly give it to them. Now, when they are adults, we need to rest from provision, making our plan that they are completely self-sustaining. With provision generally comes control—sometimes our adult children desire our provision, but they certainly don't want our control. There is absolutely nothing wrong with gifts and blessing them but continuing to provide on-going provision can enable and cripple them from being adults and the joy and confidence that brings. Housing, paychecks, insurances . . . all of these things ought to be steadily decreasing once our kids are adults, so that over the 6-years that made up each season, by age 24 they are completely on their own. Again, you are just living out the vision that was instilled in them and they have owned way back in summer! No one gets surprised.

Resting from provision doesn't mean you aren't there at various times to provide nice gifts that help them through challenging periods. This can be a real encouragement and come as a blessing and surprise relief during the inevitable bumpy roads that come in life. Also, there is nothing we enjoy more than treating our kids when we go out to dinner or taking them on trips and covering everything.

I can remember when Deb and I were married in the early years with all the kids—money was always tight, and it was such a blessing to go out to dinner with Dad and Mom and they would pick up the bill. Whew! So nice as we were trying to figure out whether this was the week for corn mush or potatoes, and there were those weeks!

So, there is the difference between blessing and crippling, between gifts and control. We want to honor them with the dignity and responsibility of them taking control of their finances and the plan and work those entail. If you continue to pay for their car or their rent or all the adult necessities, they are crippled and dependent when they nor you really want them to be. Many of these expectations should be set out during the Summer Vision Season and reinforced throughout the Fall Releasing Season.

For instance, one big area is college expectations, as I just mentioned an example of "Now That I'm 18" with our son. Many parents have different ideas on how that will work. Some parents completely save for and fund their children's entire college, and that may be a huge blessing. But then there are additional expenses—are you going to provide for all of those as well, or are you going to have them take a job to make the spending money, or book money? It is best if you plan and discuss these things in advance so that when they are adults, and go off to college, it's just normal.

We never had the funding in place for their college—we always told them we would give them free college by letting them go to Community College during their junior and senior years of high school, when they were dual-enrolled, and it was free! So, for most of them, they transferred in enough credits to cover a year or more. We worked with them to try to find whatever grants or scholarships were available and also set the expectations that they would have to work during their college as well to figure it out. They worked a lot, nanny'd, Red Lobster, valet parking, Coffee shops, and after they got out, they worked hard to pay off any loans they had. Again, we provided gifts in various ways to provide a pick-up along the way.

Deb and I have tried to invest financial gifts into our adult kids' lives at various times to give them a leg up. It wasn't ongoing support but seeking to be there and evaluate various situations as they arise and where it is inspiring and best to provide that investment. Most of this has happened in that first six years of their adult season as they are out fighting the lions, tigers, and bears in the world.

COLLEGE BOUND

A word about college; one big decision point as you are evaluating college and paying for it is whether they go to state college or private Christian University. State schools are always less expensive than private Christian schools, but the old adage "you get what you pay for" may have never been truer. Our opinion after observing a lot of situations is that it is well worth it to go to a Christian based university over those State concentrations of atheism and all that goes with it. Now, that is our opinion, and you can find examples on both sides of that where things worked well or didn't. You get to choose, but the power of the authority figures over your newly minted adult children is massive—atheistic professors mocking Christianity in philosophy and the open hedonism encouraged on campus can really serve to harden and move them towards life-style decisions that are difficult to return from.

We actually feel it is better to let them experience the godless state environment while they are in high school during their junior and senior years, where you can still talk through what they are experiencing together while they are at home and help them recognize what they are dealing with (recall our daughter and the naked man in art class). Then giving them a Christian world-view undergraduate experience, where they are encouraged by Christian professors and counselors towards a biblical worldview and lifestyle launches them off in the best way possible as young adults. If it was a choice between public high school and Christian college or vise-versa, we would choose the former hands down. If after college postgraduate fields are sought at masters or doctoral level in specializations, then perhaps secular schools are less of an issue, partly because they are now fully grounded in their adult worldview by age 24 or so.

With so many choices and on-line options, there are many ways to access Christian universities today that didn't exist even a few years ago. Also, you have to evaluate even the need and certainly the timing for college. It is never too late; I can definitely attest to that. I didn't begin my college experience until I was 31, married with five kids. That is partly where the cornmeal and potatoes came in. It is certainly easier directly out of high school, but it can always still be done.

One thing that is important for us to teach and model for our kids is that learning, and education are life-long, not just for the teens and early twenties! It may be better for them to wait a few years or take technical schooling. Just putting them into the State Lion's Den because it's "that time" and cheaper, may not be the right option—or at least the right time. Now, there have been occasions where people come out of lion's dens just fine, Daniel comes to mind and with God all things are possible. Satan is a roaring lion, prowling around seeking whom he may devour—he is also disguised as an angel of light. The combination concentrates on university campuses, disguised as professors and students. While I'm sure you know people who have come out the other side with a vibrant faith intact, the much more common story is that when the kids left home and went off to university, they left both their faith and church behind—devoured. Just don't send them there naively. As parents, we have a lot to say about where they go.

QUESTIONS FOR DISCUSSION

1. What are examples where you have had to rest from responsibility? Why is completely giving up responsibility for them difficult?

2. Can you think of examples where you still try to control your adult children?

3. What passions or interests would you like to pursue during your children's late teens and early adult years that may make releasing and resting easier for you?

4. What is the difference in continuing unhealthy provision for your adult children and blessing them with gifts? Why would one hinder them, and another encourage and empower them?

5. What are your thoughts around the effects of Christian versus secular university as discussed in the chapter?

CHAPTER 19

FRIENDSHIP

Now, during winter, you get the great reward of friendship with your adult children. While you are always their parent, your job of "parenting" is over and you choose to view them as peers, intentionally treating them as you would a good friend. Nothing is more rewarding than to enjoy that relationship—like two nights ago when our son and daughter-in-law stopped by on New Year's Eve and we sat around and talked and then enjoyed a game of Rook—the girls against the guys. A good guide is always, "What would I do with my good friend?" Then apply that answer to your adult children; that will provide the best opportunity for friendship to blossom.

As we have released them and respect them, a natural friendship develops more and more. The more we take an interest in them, encourage them, share our own world and things we are involved in, while listening to what they are doing a wonderful thing increasingly begins to happen: A genuine friendship emerges.

Now this starts to begin already back in the middle of the teen years, but you are still their authority at that point so friendship is increasing, but still limited somewhat by your authority role in this transitioning time. You'll notice on the Changing Seasons Chart, the friendship line begins to climb from the bottom of the chart around 16 years old. During the middle of the teenage years, you are intentionally beginning to transition your authority role to a friendship. Interestingly, the Resting line on the chart doesn't begin until they are 18 and officially adults.

However, once you have completely released them and truly view them as adults and peers, because they are, now the ultimate reward is to watch a genuine friendship fully develop. Does this mean you never give advice? No, you give your friends advice at times—and you also ask your friends for advice. This two-way street is wonderful with your adult kids. Also, the more comfortable they feel, the more they may ask for your advice, and then you can share it. As you are "resting" from the controls of parenting, you are opening the door wider for friendship.

Once again, this is so easy to get completely backwards, as we have seen in so many instances throughout this book. There is a lot of pressure for parents to be their young kids' friends—trying to be buddies and peers. Sadly, again this is the right thing at the wrong time. It's not your job to be your four-year-old or your nine-year-old's friend—it's completely your job to be their parent. Loving them, having fun, and doing those things that are always in season—but you aren't their friend. You are their authority and their dad or mom. But here is the beautiful thing, if we have patiently focused on the proper activities during their season, now when they are adults you have the best opportunity to enjoy a life-long friendship in the healthiest, most rewarding way possible. Look forward to it. Enjoy it. Watch it unfold.

Now in this winter season, to whatever extent you haven't released them and rested from your control, you will notice they will have less interest in being your friend. They often won't naturally gravitate towards that misplaced control; they will gravitate away. This is a real learning curve for both of you, because again the roles have switched for you from authority/dependent to interdependent peers. Remember that Power-Influence graph? At this point, all you have is your influence. You have no power at all. Now *your children choose* to what extent your influence draws them in to a relationship. They are always called to honor their parents—but not obey. And if at this point, we as parents are trying to enforce obedience, we are out of line—and probably not having much of an opportunity to practice that hobby because they are increasingly absent!

But the more we learn to "keep our mouth shut and the welcome mat out" during the transition from fall to winter, the more we will be able to enjoy the friendship as a lasting reward of that winter season. If it sounds like we've experienced this, you are right. I sometimes feel like we are pretty clumsy—but we try to keep failing forward; It is challenging but also very rewarding.

PARENT OR FRIEND?

A good book that brought out a lot of helpful aspects to being friends with your adult children is *Parent or Friend: Transitioning from Parent to Friend with your Adult Child* by Mary Ann Froehlich. In this section, I will utilize and summarize here some of the stories and concepts she really unpacks well, showing why you don't treat your young children as friends, but that you are continually laying the foundation blocks for a lifelong friendship later. Increasingly as the children transition through the Fall Harvest Season, providing the mutual respect that encourages them, and ultimately letting go completely will give the best opportunity for friendship.

She shared an example of a man named Michael whom his mother always pampered and enabled as a favorite child. As Michael grew, he struggled with his addictions, temper, relationships, finances and legal problems. His sisters would watch as their parents coddled him, bailing him out of endless problems. His sisters became successful independent women. Interestingly, Michael wasn't his sister's friend, his sisters weren't their parents' friends, and while Michael and his parents were inseparable, they were not friends. While that type of scenario is too common, it doesn't have to be. There you see the example of misplaced provision that hinders friendship—not just with Michael but the others as well. They become upset at their parents not cutting the umbilical cord. Sometimes the parents are the only ones who don't see it!

The most important thing to becoming your adult children's friend according to Froehlich as well is this: "The key to having great friendships with your adult children is to treat them as you would treat any close friend" (Froehlich, pg. 98). Always ask yourself the question, "Would I do this with my close friend, ____?" "Would I say this to my close friend, ____?" If your best friend was behind on her credit card bills, would you pay them? If the friendship is healthy, you would listen and encourage, but you wouldn't pay it. We respect our friends' schedules. When we see them, we don't say, "Your hair looks awful." We don't text our friends to make sure they got up in the morning. When we rescue adults, or continue to treat them like children, we are telling them that we do not trust them. Learning to treat your adult kids as friends is critical to them actually becoming friends.

A 28-year-old woman who has always been "Daddy's girl" and is still getting financed for her hearts every desire may feel close, but they are not friends. A 35-year-old man who lives with his mother, having an enmeshed dependent relationship where she takes care of him, and he is her companion do not enjoy a healthy friendship. Strange dynamics and resentments build in those scenarios (The examples in this section are from Froehlich, Pgs. 97-100).

I have noticed that when adult children continue to be housed and coddled by their parents, they have the "luxury" of obsessing over minor things. They actually get less confident and may take four times as long on certain appearances or details. While they may be able to reach level 30,000 in Minecraft, they can't seem to sort out the major issues from the minor details. Appearances, details, or even Minecraft are not bad, but when you add those adult interruptions like electric bills, rent, grocery bills, or roof maintenance, they can really throw your game off. When adult children are truly released and expected to take care of themselves, then the sheer weight of the responsibility sifts the priorities and brings the real man or woman out. Along with that comes dignity and confidence that we can come up beside as friends and peers to cheer on.

We hear Genesis 2:24 where it states that a man shall leave his father and mother, and we tend to think of this in the context of marriage, which is true. But particularly, for a son, the closer he has been to his mother, the more that umbilical cord needs to be severed when he is an adult. The closer the relationship that they enjoyed, the more difficult that can be—particularly for Mom. As parents with sons know, once they leave you often hear from them much less than daughters, however, once the cord is firmly cut and maturity has happened, often the communication improves.

By learning to rest from the parts of parenting that we have been so accustomed to like responsibility, control, provision, and then learning to treat them like trusted friends, this truly can be a most rewarding season.

FRIENDSHIP REWARD

As you allow your adult children to find their own wings and make their own path, and as you get through particularly those first six years of that Winter Season, hopefully that friendship will continue to solidify. As they become more confident in who they are, they will often start to see and appreciate the values you have instilled more personally for themselves.

We recently experienced this with our family. When the kids were at home, we would have family devotions at the dinner table or at bedtime; it wasn't always consistent, but it was a value we tried to instill. Then, as all of our kids were adults, at different times we would all take family vacations together and I would try to find a time where we could all at least have a meal together and at times we would do a family devotion or Bible discussion. As the kids grew and in-laws and grandkids came, this became less frequent.

A few weeks ago, one of our daughters contacted all of her siblings and invited all of them to come over for a special evening specifically for sharing what God has been doing in each of their lives, a special passage of Scripture that was meaningful, and what plan or method each has been using to be in God's Word; that type of thing. Everyone shared together and encouraged each other. It was the most rewarding time to be included and not instigating—in fact, my daughter said, "Dad, try to keep it on the down-low" so I didn't take the *teacher* position. Everyone was encouraged and they are working out a schedule to do this regularly; they are all in the fight together, iron sharpening iron, helping each other in the battle of life.

Another example was that we just had the family all over for Easter and we always have a family egg hunt where we hide eggs all over the yard with candy inside and turn the grandkids loose. We have this carton of "Resurrection Eggs" that has a dozen eggs and by opening them in order, you tell the story. The first one has a little palm branch in it, the second silver pieces, the third a little towel, whip, crown of thorns, etc. The last egg is empty symbolizing the empty tomb that we always go through with the grandkids.

I was exhausted from a huge Sunday and Deb and I were discussing doing it and I was just not up for going through the 12 eggs of Easter (I have trouble listening through the 12 Days of Christmas too). I said, "Let's just forget it." I'm thinking surely one year without going through the Resurrection Eggs isn't the end of the world! Interestingly though, one of our other adult kids decided to take it on themselves to pull all the grandkids together and go through the whole thing with them. Again, it was a pleasure to just sit back and observe those values—that we had tried to instill, being owned and now passed on by their own initiative.

Over time, as the kids grow and work out life, knocking against challenges and people, it is the most rewarding thing of all to enjoy one another's company and friendship as adults and as equals, and all the more if they have a personal value in God's Word and faith in Jesus. Just this morning I spent a few hours with one of my adult daughters because she asked if I wanted to get my nails done with her. (Now this is Deb, in case you were concerned) Then we grabbed a drink at Starbucks together while she helped me download the Starbucks app to start earning rewards. The true reward is that she wanted to be with me. She invited me. It doesn't get better than this. Enjoy your new friendships with your adult kids. There truly is no greater joy!

QUESTIONS FOR DISCUSSION

1. What are some examples of having a good friendship with your adult child?

2. What are the things that will hinder a friendship with your adult children?

3. We discussed on the Changing Seasons Chart, when Friendship starts and when Rest starts? When were they and what would be the reasons they would begin at different times?

4. When should you give advice to your adult children?

5. Do you think you still have power, control, or authority over your children after they have become adults? Why or why not?

6. Would your adult children say you are still trying to control them and their decisions?

CHAPTER 20

THE ULTIMATE REWARD

By seeking to best do the right thing in the right season, we work in rhythm with God's created design and seek to steward that trust of raising godly children the best we can. While there are many many factors that we cannot control or even understand, if you jump into the season you are in with your children, and do what Paul said, "forgetting what is behind and straining towards what is ahead, I press on towards the mark . . ." Phil. 3:13 we can find the greatest reward possible in parenting! God has so much grace in parenting and kids are very resilient. Nobody gets it right all of the time, but if you can understand the proper thing at the proper time and do the best you can during that season, just be patient—you may yet be amazed at the ultimate reward that awaits you with your children: a true friend to learn from, lean on, and lock arms with as you both follow the Lord!

TRANSITIONING PARENTING TO GOD

I have come to really appreciate Hebrews 12:10, particularly during the Fall Harvest and Winter Reward season: "Our fathers disciplined us for *a short time* as they thought best, but God disciplines us for our good." It is so easy to look back and analyze and regret this or that. You recognize so many areas you could have done better or differently. We've definitely done this. But I just love this perspective, "Our fathers disciplined us for a short time as they thought best . . ." And guess what—we did too, and so did you! We all do as we think is best. It is the rare parent that says, "I really want to mess my kid up!" Of course not. We all have different backgrounds, different circumstances and temperaments, but we did what we knew, the best we knew and now it's done. And then here is the beautiful part, "But God disciplines us for our good."

In a real sense, part of the *Rest* in this season is that we truly hand them over to God and let Him teach them now, discipline them now, direct them now. We did our part—the best we knew during each season, but God will discipline them for their good. Now of course, we give them to God all through their lives, and pray pray pray, but this is a different level. They are now adults, and our role of parenting has shifted. We're always their parent—but now we step aside in many areas and responsibilities. We enjoy their friendship, celebrate their victories, weep with them during the hard times, but truly recognize that God is their Father, and this is what we have been raising them towards all along! He is always working, and He has it handled. We can rest in that!

Thank you so much for taking the time to read and process this. Deb and I pray the greatest abundant harvest of God on you, your children, and your children's children to 1,000 generations!

Happy farming.

QUESTIONS FOR DISCUSSION

1. How does Hebrews 12:10 make you feel?

2. As parents, you've always trusted your children to God, but how is it different to release them to the Father's care once they are adults?

3. Now that you have finished the book, what are one or two things that stand out the most to you for your parenting journey?

4. Which of the four seasons spoke the most to you? Why?

Our family; the adults from left to right with a bit about their lives:

Saul & Heather Rapalo, Juliet (4) & Celeste (1): Saul and Heather met at Moody Bible Institute. Saul had led youth ministry, and was currently managing at Panther Coffee. Saul was actively involved in their church as a small group leader before he suddenly died of a brain aneurism at just 36 years old, six months ago. Devastated, Heather thankfully has an amazingly caring church family and friends as she tries to navigate her new path. She has a master's degree in social work and is a licensed mental health counselor. She was serving as a counselor at the Foundation Counseling Center prior to Saul's passing. Heather lives in Miami with her two little girls, Juliet 4, and Celeste 1.

Alecia Fiechter: Alecia graduated with a bachelor's degree in music from Moody Bible Institute. She now runs her own music business called Joy Music Studios, where she inspires others to reach their full potential in music. More information can be found at joymusicstudios.com. Alecia has been to nearly 20 countries sharing Christ's love through music and ministries around the world. She now resides in her home in St. Cloud, Florida. Alecia also has a side rental business, renting her three extra bedrooms to other professionals, who've become like family.

Justin & Shelby Fiechter, Tessa (6), Emmie (4), & Myles (2): Justin is a roof salesman for Covenant Roofing and Shelby is busy with their three kids and leads The Connection Kids ministry. They met in Africa and after they were married, spent two years there serving in the squatter camps of Johannesburg. They live in St Cloud and Justin currently serves in our local church and strives to lead and love his family while balancing family, work, and ministry.

Micah Fiechter: Micah also graduated from Moody Bible Institute and works for Culture Amp, helping companies improve employee productivity and satisfaction. He is currently working on launching Prayer Houses: a platform seeking to mobilize corporate prayer inside homes, apartments and dorm rooms in America. Micah lives in Chicago and has been attending Axess Church, a recent church plant and is also part of the International House of Prayer.

Joey & Leah Waddell: Tyler (9), Rylee (7), Austin (6) & Shaya (4): Joey graduated from Liberty University with a degree in Web Technology and Design and Leah from Southeastern University, with a degree in Theology and Ministry Arts. They spent a year in Guatemala, and currently live in St Cloud. Joey works for Disney as a platform engineer. Leah is busy with four children, Monat Haircare and serves in the Connection Worship Ministry.

Rick & Deb: Rick and Deb and their family moved from Indiana to St. Cloud FL in 2005 to plant The Connection Church where Rick serves as Lead Pastor. He currently serves on the Chamber of Commerce board and Council on Aging board where their church meets. He also serves with a Global Alliance for Church Multiplication. (GACX.io) Deb leads the Women's Connect Ministry and continues to be involved with counseling and hospitality ministry. Her life is full and blessed with her kids and grandkids. Rick and Deb also own a real estate rental company to help with funding. Whenever possible, they enjoy getting away on their "35th Anniversary Special," a newer Road Glide that replaced the tired 22-year-old Kawasaki Vulcan.

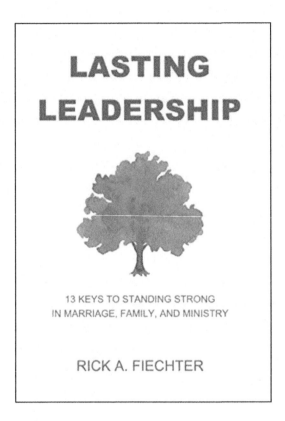

Lasting Leadership was Rick's prior book based on a real-world case study that uncovered 13 keys that helped pastors plant churches and continue leading them for up to 33 years while they grew to over 1,500 people. At the time of the study, these pastors were all in their 60's, still enjoying ministry, happy marriages, and children who were all following the Lord. This study set out to discover keys that helped that happen.

Starting is easy, finishing well seems much harder. By learning and applying these principles to your life in any context, these keys may help you discover this unique combination to enjoy a life of lasting leadership.

APPENDIX A

BOOK AND MEDIA RECOMMENDATIONS FOR SEASONS:

Season 1: Spring Planting: Heart & Obedience. (0-6)

Spanking: a Loving Discipline by Roy Lessin
Shepherding Your Child's Heart by Tedd Trip
The Power of Praying for Your Children by Stormie Omartian
The Five Love Languages of Children by Gary Chapman

Season 2: Summer Cultivating: Teaching & Vision. (7-12)

Adventures in Odyssey
Super Book
The Greatest Adventures—Stories from the Bible
Story Keepers
Stories of the Bible (YouTube)
Listener Kids (YouTube)
New City Catechism
Uncle Arthur's Bedtime Stories
The Tech-wise Family by Andy and Amy Crouch
Refuel: The Complete New Testament for Guys (Biblezeens)
Refuel: Epic Battles of the Old Testament, Nelson Bible
Raising a Modern-Day Knight by Robert Lewis
Money Savvy Pig on Amazon

Season 3: Fall Harvest: Encourage & Release. (13-17)

The Blessing by Gary Smalley
Wild at Heart by John Eldridge
That's My Teenage Son by Rick Johnson
Making Children Mind Without Losing Yours by Kevin Leman

Season 4: Winter Reward: Friendship & Rest. (18+)

Doing Life with your Adult Children by Jim Burns
Parent or Friend? by Mary Ann Froehlich

APPENDIX B

Charts

Power & Influence Graph

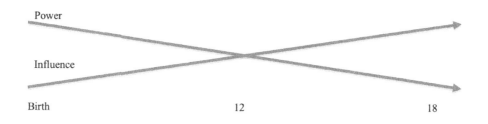

Changing Seasons Chart

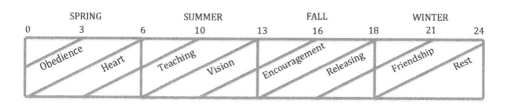

SEASONS OF PARENTING

APPENDIX C

Man of the Sword &
Princess of the Rings
Reports

1. Read the appropriate Bible passages that talk about the particular Man of the Sword you are studying.

2. Write a report putting in your own words all the different aspects of the Man of the Sword's life. Include details but don't copy word for word out of the Bible.

3. Evaluate the specific S.W.O.R.D. characteristics in the Man of the Sword's life.

   S. Servant: In what ways did he demonstrate being a servant in his life? In what ways didn't he demonstrate it?

   W. Wisdom: In what areas did he show wisdom? In what areas didn't he show wisdom?

   O. Obedience: In what specific ways did he obey God? In what areas didn't he obey God? What were the consequences?

   R. Respect: To whom and in what ways did he show respect? Where didn't he show respect?

D. Determination: Did he show determination? If so, how did he? Where could he have been more determined?

4. Find the main characteristic of this Man of the Sword that you would like to live out in your life. Give one specific example of how you will apply this.

5. Pay attention to spelling and neatness.

Between the Old and New Testaments, there were around 50 of them. (In some cases, the magazine duplicated a character, so I picked a different one from the Bible.) So, if we took two years to do that, it averaged about one every other week. They would write out the study for the character in their notebook and then we would go out together and talk about it.

At the end of this we had a "Man of the Sword Final Thesis." Sounded like big stuff—and it was a big project for a 12-year-old. We took extra time and I edited it so that the spelling was correct and it was typed out, we put a special book report cover on it, made it look super important and official and it was a big accomplishment.

MAN OF THE SWORD
FINAL THESIS

1. Write a cover page with your name and "Man of the Sword Final Thesis" in capitals and centered on the page.

2. Write a clear definition of each of the qualities: Servanthood means . . .

3. Find the best Bible passage that teaches that quality and write the verse(s)

4. Go through all of your studies and find the 4 best examples of Servanthood and write a paragraph or two summarizing why he was the best at that.

5. Go through all of your studies and find the 2 worst examples of Servanthood and write a paragraph or two summarizing why he was the worst at it.

6. Think carefully about the subject and write 4 goals for yourself that you want to demonstrate in living out servanthood through your teenage years and beyond.

7. Do the same for all five qualities.

8. Finally, write a paragraph or two on how you will treat girls in a godly manner and then end with 4 goals for how you will live with girls through your teenage years.

Writing qualities:

15 – 20 pages total
Page numbers bottom right
Typewritten, double-spaced
Words must be spelled right—if you don't know, look them up in the dictionary
Turn in first draft by March 1
You will probably do 3 drafts before it is perfect.

Then all of this culminated in a "Man of the Sword Ceremony" where we got each of the boys their own sword. We got Justin "Peter's Sword" from *Lord of the Rings* and Micah got the "Sword of

Solomon." We planned this formal ceremony on their 13th birthday and invited special friends. Here is a copy of the invitation sent out for Justin:

MAN OF THE SWORD CEREMONY INVITATION

MAN OF THE SWORD

Dear Danny & Terri,

This is a special invitation to invite you to a "Man of the Sword" ceremony. What's that? This is a ceremony that Justin has been preparing for over the last 2 ½ years. He has read the New Testament and Epic Battle Stories from the Old Testament and completed nearly 50 "Man of the Sword" studies of godly men in the Bible who fought the battle well.

S.W.O.R.D is an acronym for Servant-hood, Wisdom, Obedience, Respect, and Determination; all qualities in varying degrees that these men demonstrated and that Justin wants to learn to apply to his own life as he takes the journey from boyhood to manhood.

If you've lived very long, you realize that life is a battle! In fact, Ephesians says that we are in an all-out war with the powers of darkness, so we'd better learn to fight. Ephesians also commands us to take the Sword of the Spirit, which is the Word of God as our offensive weapon against our enemy, the devil. We must learn to wield it well as we fight the fight.

Justin compiled a list of special people he would like to have share this exciting evening with and you are on that list. It will be a night with video, sharing, refreshments, and some godly men speaking into Justin's life. He will be presented with his actual sword, and his special copy of the Sword of the Spirit. We would really love to have you join us!

This will be on Justin's 13th Birthday, **Sunday, August 24th at 7:00pm** at the Barney Veal Center located behind McDonalds just west of the Turn Pike entrance in Kissimmee. Please let us know if you can come! 407-957-3358 or **debfiechter@hotmail.com**

Hope to see you there!

Rick & Deb Fiechter

PRINCESS OF THE RINGS

This Study was originally designed for my daughter as a dad and daughter time, a way for me to train her up in the Lord. She started this when she was 11 and finished when she was 13 (we designed it to coincide with her birthday). After my daughter finished the study, she then wrote an 11-page paper sharing what she learned and laid out the goals she believed God wanted for her life. Together we discussed the five characteristics of a Princess of The Rings. For her birthday I gave her a promise ring symbolizing the commitments she made in her paper and promising her that I would walk with her through each step.

This study is a great way for a dad and daughter to grow their relationship or for a mom and daughter. It is very adaptable to any situation you may need. The study can be done in a short time, or you can take the two years that we did. We chose approximately 20 women in the Bible to study. Each character study can be done in order or study the ones you want to learn about the most. The main point is to get into scripture and allow God to make you into the woman he wants you to be. (Thomas Todd)

A PRINCESS IS BORN

Princess of The Rings is a Bible study that will take you through the entire Bible. While reading you will study character qualities from many women throughout Bible. The purpose of this study is to help young women develop the character qualities that are typical of a daughter of God, a daughter of the King, which makes her a princess! Today's culture sells us a very different picture from the picture God has given us in his Word. We are told through media that we should be seductive or focus mainly on beauty secrets to try to attract a man. This study hopes to help young women get back to the picture God has for us. The picture God gives us is a Proverbs 31 woman.

There are five main qualities that we will concentrate on in scripture and these five qualities are the traits we will study from the women in the Bible and also see in the life of Christ. The acronym comes from our title, Princess of The Rings. R.I.N.G.S. stands for:

R. Resolute: A woman of God is resolute. Resolute is defined as having determination or characterized by determination. Often, we are taught that godly women are weak and passive, this is not true. Scriptures utilized are Proverbs 31:15-17 and 1 Cor. 1:27-29

I. Insightful (wisdom): A woman of God has insight. She is wise. Insightful/Wisdom is defined as having good sense, making wise decisions, perceptiveness, clear perception, self-awareness, and good judgment. Proverbs 31:26; 2:6; 3:13, and James 1:5.

N. Noble Servant: A woman of God is a Noble Servant, a servant to the King of Kings and the Lord of Lords. A servant is defined as a person devoted to another or to a cause, creed, etc. Servant is also defined as one who serves. The idea is living our life for the Lord and not for ourselves. Also, the idea is to put others needs before our needs. All of Proverbs 31 seems to define a servant. The end of Proverbs 31 says she fears the Lord, this is a clear sign of a servant of the Lord and is central to a Princess of the King. Mat 20:26-28, 1 Cor. 13.

G. Godly/Pure: A woman of God is godly and pure. Purity is important as a daughter of the King. Let's define these words also. Godly means to be devoted to God. Pure means to be free from anything that messes it up and pure means to keep oneself from sex before marriage. So, our definition consists of combining both of the previous definitions, to be godly/pure is to be devoted to God and saving ourselves for marriage. The proverbs 31 woman clearly is a woman who is devoted to God and has saved herself for her husband. God desires a relationship with us that is the deepest form of love we can know. You may have been hurt in this area in your past or you may be reading this and have already messed up when it comes to purity, it is not too late. Don't believe the lie that you can never be good in this area so who cares. God cares and he offers you total forgiveness for wherever you have been and whatever you have done. 1 John 1:7-10.

S. Submissive: A woman of God is submissive. Submissive is not a doormat, not someone to be walked on or always told what to do. Submissive is not following someone who abuses you and controls all you do. Biblical submission is defined as yielding control to God, surrendering to God, obeying God in what we do.

Made in the USA
Columbia, SC
23 June 2023

18770233R00163